Skillbuilder Workbook

for

Beebe, Beebe, and Redmond

Interpersonal Communication
Relating to Others

Fifth Edition

prepared by

Mark V. Redmond
Iowa State University

PEARSON

Boston   New York   San Francisco
Mexico City   Montreal   Toronto   London   Madrid   Munich   Paris
Hong Kong   Singapore   Tokyo   Cape Town   Sydney

ISBN-13: 978-0-205-52452-5
ISBN-10:   0-205-52452-4

Printed in the United States of America

10 9 8 7 6 5 4 3 2 1   11 10 09 08 07

CONTENTS

PREFACE

This Study Guide contains 137 activities and exercises designed to help the student understand the principles and develop competency in the use of the communication concepts introduced in *Interpersonal Communication: Relating to Others, 5th Edition.* The activities are arranged by chapter so that the student can do the activities outside of class to practice skills and to develop awareness of the concepts as they are introduced in the text and in class.

The exercises in this study guide focus on application and analysis of the concepts discussed in the text. It is important for the student to connect the text information to his or her own life. By doing so, the student can see the relevancy of the material and will be motivated to learn. Most exercises are followed by questions to encourage critical thinking and analysis about the exercise and the application to "real" relationships. The exercises may be required by the instructor as a graded assignment or used to stimulate discussion in class. Assigning the exercises prior to the class discussion of the concepts gives students the opportunity to enter class discussions with well-prepared examples.

The best activities and exercises from the previous editions have been retained. New activities and exercises have been added that parallel changes in the latest edition of the text itself. In addition, various activities and exercises have been revised to insure student understanding and a heightened learning experience.

In the attempt to make this study guide "user friendly" for the student, Study Questions and Vocabulary Flash Cards are included for each chapter. The questions serve as a review for each chapter to help the student prepare for tests. The flash cards aid the student in learning the vocabulary words for clear understanding of the communication concepts discussed in class and on tests.

ACKNOWLEDGEMENT

Kay E. Muller established the foundation of this workbook for the first two editions of the text. I am grateful to her for creating a successful framework and for identifying many invaluable activities and exercises that continue to be used.

CHAPTER 1
INTRODUCTION TO INTERPERSONAL
COMMUNICATION

OBJECTIVES

After studying the material in this chapter *Interpersonal Communication: Relating to Others*, and completing the exercises in this section of the study guide, you should understand:

1. The difference between the definitions of communication, human communication, and interpersonal communication.
2. Why it is useful to study interpersonal communication.
3. Communication as action, interaction, and transaction.
4. The key components of the communication process.
5. Computer mediated communication as interpersonal communication.
6. The impact of the Internet on interpersonal relationships.
7. The five principles of interpersonal communication.
8. The four myths about interpersonal communication, and
9. The strategies, which can improve your interpersonal communication competence.

STUDY QUESTIONS

You should be able to answer the following questions:

1. What are the components of the definition of interpersonal communication?
2. What are the four reasons we should study interpersonal communication?
3. What is meant by human communication as action, interaction, and transaction?
4. How does mediated interpersonal communication differ from face-to-face?
5. What are the five principles of interpersonal communication?
6. What does it mean that interpersonal communication is governed by rules?
7. What are the four myths about interpersonal communication?
8. What are the six ways to improve your interpersonal communication competence?

EXERCISE 1.1 THE IMPORTANCE OF INTERPERSONAL COMMUNICATION IN YOUR LIFE

Purposes:
1. To increase your awareness of how interpersonal communication affects your relationships with family.
2. To increase your awareness of how interpersonal communication affects your relationships with friends.

Directions:
1. Think about a relationship with a family member and a relationship with a friend that has improved over the last few years.
2. Write their first names in the appropriate spots.
3. Answer the corresponding questions.

FAMILY MEMBER: (first name) _____

What changes have taken place in the relationship?

_____

_____

_____

What interpersonal communication skills of you or the other person have improved in the last few years?

_____

_____

_____

How have the changes in the communication skills affected the relationship?

_____

_____

_____

What changes still need to occur in either of your interpersonal communication skills to further improve the relationship?

_____

_____

_____

FRIEND: (first name) _____

What changes have taken place in the relationship?

_____

_____

_____

What changes have occurred in the interpersonal communication skills of you or the other person?

_____

_____

_____

How have the changes in the communication skills affected the relationship?

_____

_____

_____

What changes still need to occur in either of your interpersonal communication skills to further improve the relationship?

_____

_____

_____

Questions

1. What interpersonal communication skills have changed in you that are common to both relationships?

2. In what ways have the problems encountered in either relationship been related to ineffective interpersonal communication skills?

EXERCISE 1.2   NOISE IN YOUR COMMUNICATION

Purposes:
1. To recognize how noise is interfering in your daily communication.
2. To identify various sources of noise.
3. To help you understand how noise relates to the models of communication.

Directions:
1. For this exercise you are to identify two examples in your day that can be used to illustrate the various ways that noise has interfered in your communication.
2. Remember that noise is anything literal or psychological that interferes with the clear reception and interpretation of a message.

Noise in the Source (How have you created noise as you developed messages today?)
   1.

   2.

Noise in the Receiver (How has someone who was listening to you be affected by noise within themselves?)
   1.

   2.

Noise in the Channel (What kinds of noise has interfered with messages between the source and the receiver?)
   1.

   2.

Noise in the Message (What aspects of any messages today created misunderstandings?)
   1.

   2.

Questions:
1. Which occurrence of noise created the greatest problems? Which the least?

2. How might you best overcome each source of noise or minimize its impact?

EXERCISE 1.3   **REALIZING YOUR COMMUNICATION STRENGTHS AND WEAKNESSES**

Purposes:
1.   To recognize your strong areas of communication.
2.   To recognize areas of communication in which you need to improve.
3.   To understand how you become aware on your interpersonal communication strengths and your areas that need improvement.

Directions:
1.   List three of your interpersonal communication strengths.
2.   List three interpersonal communication areas that you think need the most improvement.

STRENGTHS

1._____

2._____

3._____

AREAS TO IMPROVE

1._____

2._____

3._____

Questions:
1.   How do you know you have these strengths? What kind of feedback do you get from others? How have your experiences with others confirmed that you do these things well?

2.   How do you know you need to improve in these areas? What kind of feedback do you get from others? How have your experiences with others confirmed that you need to work on these areas?

EXERCISE 1.4   **COMPUTER MEDIATED INTERPERSONAL COMMUNICATION COMPARED TO FACE-TO-FACE INTERPERSONAL COMMUNICATION**

Purposes:
1. To explore how computer mediated communication (CMC) differs from face-to-face (FtF) interpersonal communication.
2. To compare computer mediated relationships to face-to-face relationships.

Directions:
1. Reflect on CMC and FtF interactions with friends, acquaintances, and strangers.
2. Evaluate CMC and FtF communication according to the four differences discussed in the text.

Four Differences
COMPARE CMC AND FtF INTERACTIONS IN TERMS OF:

1A. Anonymity. How does not knowing or barely knowing an online partner affect interactions? _____

_____

1B. Anonymity: How does not knowing or barely knowing a partner in face-to-face interactions affect those interactions? _____

_____

2A. Physical Appearance: In what ways does the lack of physical appearance affect on-line interactions? _____

_____

2B. Physical Appearance: In what ways does the presence of physical appearance affect face-to-face interactions? _____

_____

3.   Distance: How does distance affect your CMC and FtF interactions differently?

_____

_____

4A. Time: To what degree do delays in responding affect the meaning of the messages you receive online? _____

_____

4B. Time: To what degree do delays in responding affect the meaning of the messages you receive in FtF interactions? _____

_____

EXERCISE 1.5   TV BINGO WITH PRINCIPLES OF INTERPERSONAL COMMUNICATION

Purposes:
1. To understand the principles of interpersonal communication.
2. To be able to identify the principles in interactions.

Directions:
1. For this activity you are to find examples from TV shows of each of the five principles of interpersonal communication covered in the text.
2. Familiarize yourself with the five principles so that you can readily identify them if you see them.
3. You can focus on one principle and try to find an example, or after watching a couple of programs, go over the five principles and see if any of them were readily apparent in the episodes you watched
4. Do some channel surfing, focusing on TV shows in which interpersonal relationships are important (e. g. *Friends, How I Met Your Mother, Desperate Housewives, The O.C.*) or watch for examples in any TV programs you normally view.
5. Record the TV show, character, and event that provide the requested example.
6. See how quickly you can fill in all five principles to achieve "BINGO!"

Principles   Provide: TV Show, Characters, and Example
1. Interpersonal Communication Connects Us to Others: Find an example of interpersonal communication playing a critical role in the development of a relationship.

2. Interpersonal Communication Is Irreversible: Find an example where a character would like to or tries to take back something said or done.

3. Interpersonal Communication Is Complicated: Provide an example where misunderstanding or misinterpretation occurs because of the complexity of the message.

4. Interpersonal Communication Is Governed by Rules: Provide an example where the characters create explicit rules to govern the way they interpersonally communicate.

5. Interpersonal Communication Involves Both Content and Relationship Dimensions: List an example in which confusion about the nature of the relationship occurs because of the way messages have been interpreted.

How long did you have to watch TV to find the five examples? _____
Compare with classmates to see who won BINGO with the shortest time.

7

EXERCISE 1.6   IDENTIFYING YOUR COMMUNICATION RULES

Purposes:
1. To become aware of your personal communication rules that you expect others to follow.
2. To understand the difference between explicit and implicit communication rules.
3. To recognize how you react when your communication rules are violated.
4. To determine how you developed your communication rules.

Directions:
1. List five rules you have which govern your communication interactions with others.
2. Identify how many of the rules you have verbalized to other people with whom you communicate.
3. List the ways you react when someone violates your communication rules.
4. For each rule, state how you learned the expected behaviors.

RULES	VERBALIZED	UNVERBALIZED	REACTION	ORIGIN

EXERCISE 1.7   IDENTIFYING MYTHS THAT GUIDE YOUR INTERACTIONS

Purposes:
1. To understand how myths (commonly held misconceptions) affect our lives.
2. To identify some of the myths by which you interact with other people.

Directions:
1. Below are the myths that were identified in the text. Evaluate the degree to which you previously believed and operated under that myth.
2. Create your own set of myths (a misconception or exaggeration) that you know is false, but that you find yourself following nonetheless (for example, if I'm nice to other people, they will be nice to me).

MYTHS FROM THE TEXT
1. "More words will make the meaning clearer."

    I used to think this was: Very True

    True

    Somewhat True

    Somewhat False

    Never thought this way

2. "Meanings are in words."

    I used to think this was: Very True

    True

    Somewhat True

    Somewhat False

    Never thought this way

3. "Information equal communication."

    I used to think this was: Very True

    True

    Somewhat True

    Somewhat False

    Never thought this way

4. "Interpersonal problems are always communication problems."

    I used to think this was: Very True

    True

    Somewhat True

    Somewhat False

    Never thought this way

YOUR OWN MYTHS

1. _____

_____

_____

_____

2. _____

_____

_____

_____

3. _____

_____

_____

_____

4. _____

_____

_____

_____

_____

<u>Questions:</u>

1. In what ways do believing and behaving according to these myths undermine the effectiveness of your interpersonal communication?

_____

_____

_____

2. What can you do to overcome the impact of these myths on your relationships?

_____

_____

_____

3. What can you do when you realize that your partner is operating under some myth?

_____

_____

_____

EXERCISE 1.8   UNDERSTANDING YOUR ETHICAL COMMUNICATION

Purposes:
1. To understand the attributes of ethical interpersonal communication.
2. To become aware of your communication patterns in relation to ethical communication as described in Chapter 1 of the *Interpersonal Communication: Relating to Others.*

Directions:
1. Identify three people with whom you communicate on a daily basis.
2. Evaluate your conversations with these three people over a two-day period.
3. Summarize your findings by filling in the following chart:
    Rate your conversations for how frequently you display other-orientation, honesty, and keeping confidences according to the following scale:

    5. Always   4. Almost always   3. Sometimes   2. Almost never   1. Never

Person	Relationship	Other-Orientation	Honesty	Kiep Confidences
1.				
2.				
3.				

The higher your score is, the higher your ethical communication behavior is. Compare your scores between the different people you chose.

Questions:

1. How is your ethical behavior the same with all three people?

2. How is it different?

3. Why might your ethical communication behavior change, depending on the person and the relationship you have with that person?

Communication	Human Communication
Interpersonal Communication	Encode
Decode	Receiver
Message	Channel
Noise	Context
Feedback	Impersonal Communication

Process of making sense out of the world and sharing that sense with others by creating meaning through the use of verbal and nonverbal messages.	Process of acting upon information.
To translate ideas, feelings and thoughts into a code.	A distinctive, transactional form of human communication involving mutual influence, usually for the purpose of managing relationships.
Person who decodes a message and attempts to make sense out of what the source has encoded.	To interpret ideas, feelings, and thoughts that have been translated into a code.
Pathway through which messages are sent.	Written, spoken, and unspoken elements of communication to which people assign meaning.
Physical and psychological environment for communication.	Anything literal or psychological, that interferes with the accurate reception of a message.
Process that occurs when we treat others as objects or respond to their roles rather than to who they are as unique persons.	Response to a message.

Symbol	Relationship
Episode	Source
Mass Communication	Impersonal Communication
Public Communication	Small Group Communication
Intrapersonal Communication	Mediated Interpersonal Communication
Social Information Processing Theory	Systems Theory

Connection established with another person through communication.	A representation of something else.
Originator of a thought or emotion, who puts it into a code that can be understood by a receiver.	A sequence of interactions between individuals, during which the message of one person influences the message of another
Communication that occurs when we treat people as objects, or when we respond to their role, rather than whom they are as a unique person.	Process that occurs when one person issues the same message to many people at once; the creator of the message is usually not physically present, and there is virtually no opportunity for listeners to respond immediately to the speaker.
Process that occurs when a group of from three to fifteen people meet to interact with a common purpose and mutually influence one another.	Process that occurs when a speaker addresses a large audience in person.
Communication with others established or maintained through media (such as e-mail, telephones, or faxes) rather than through face-to-face encounters.	Communication with yourself; thinking.
Theory that describes the interconnected elements of a system in which change in one element affects all the other elements.	Theory that suggests people can communicate relational and emotional messages via the Internet, although such messages take longer to express without nonverbal cues.

Content	Communibiological Approach
Rule	Ethics
Symbol	Relationship Dimension
Social Learning Theory	Egocentric Communicator
Other-Oriented Communicator	Asynchronous Interaction
Hyperpersonal Communication	Cues-Filtered-Out Theory

Theoretical perspective that suggests communication behavior can be predicted based on personal traits and characteristics that result from our genetic or biological background.	Information, ideas, or suggested actions that a speaker wishes to share.
Beliefs, values, and moral principles by which we determine what is right or wrong.	Followable prescription that indicates what behavior is obligated, preferred, or prohibited in certain contexts.
The implied aspect of a communication message, which conveys information about emotions, attitudes, power, and control.	Word, sound, or visual image that represents something else, such as a thought, concept, or object.
A person who creates messages without giving much thought to the person who is listening: a communicator who is self-focused and self-absorbed.	Theory of human behavior that suggests we can learn how to adapt and adjust our behavior toward others; how we behave is not solely dependent on our genetic or biological makeup
Process in which messages are not necessarily read, heard, or seen at the time you send them; there may be a time delay between when you send a message and when it is received.	One who considers the thoughts, feelings, and perspectives of communication partners while maintaining his or her own integrity.
Theory that suggests that communication of emotions is restricted when people send messages to others via e-mail because nonverbal cues such as facial expression and tone of voice are filtered out.	A certain type of interpersonal communication that is facilitated by using a computer to establish relationships with others.

Media Richness Theory	Metacommunication
Emotional Response Theory	

Verbal or nonverbal communication about communication.	Theory that identifies the richness of a communication medium based on the amount of information, including emotional expression, it communicates.
	Theory that suggests any human emotion experienced can be interpreted along three dimensions: 1) pleasure-displeasure, 2) arousal-nonarousal, and 3) dominance-submissiveness. Our emotional response to what we experience helps determine whether we ultimately approach or avoid what we are experiencing.

CHAPTER 2
INTERPERSONAL COMMUNICATION
AND SELF

OBJECTIVES

After studying the material in this chapter of *Interpersonal Communication: Relating to Others* and completing the exercises in this section of the study guide, you should understand:

1. The difference between self-concept and self-esteem.
2. How your attitudes, beliefs, and values shape your behavior and self-image.
3. How self-concept is developed through interaction with others, association with groups, the roles we assume, and self labels.
4. How to improve your self-esteem.
5. Two models of self-disclosure.
6. The characteristics of self-disclosure.

STUDY QUESTIONS

You should be able to answer the following questions:

1. What is the difference between self-concept and self-esteem?
2. What are attitudes, beliefs, and values? How do they relate to self-concept?
3. What are the three dimensions of self?
4. What are the four factors that contribute to the development of self-concept?
5. Define and explain each of the strategies for improving your self-esteem?
6. How does self-concept and self-esteem affect interpersonal communication and relationships?
7. Explain what communication style means.
8. Explain the Johari window and social penetration.
9. What are the characteristics of self-disclosure?

EXERCISE 2.1   BELIEFS, VALUES, AND ATTITUDES

Purposes:
1. To understand whom you are.
2. To identify how beliefs, attitudes, and values make up a part of your self.

Directions:
Complete the following sentence stems:

Values:

I value_____

I value_____

I value _____

Beliefs:

I believe _____

I believe _____

I believe _____

Attitudes:

I like_____

I like_____

I like_____

Questions:

1. Which of the things that you identified has the greatest impact on your interactions with other people?

2. Which of the things that you identified has been the newest quality that you've added to your self?

3. Which of the things has been part of who you are the longest?

4. How do these values, beliefs, and attitudes compare to those held by your parents?

5. How do these values, beliefs, and attitudes compare to those held by your closest friend?

EXERCISE 2.2   FINDING YOUR UNIQUENESS

Purpose:

1. To help you realize the qualities you possess that make you who you are.

Directions:

1. Think about each of the following questions.
2. Write down your initial impressions or thoughts for each question. BE HONEST!!

---

1. Write three positive words that describe you.

   (1) _____ (2) _____ (3) _____

2. What single factor contributes most to your self-esteem? Why?

   _____

   _____

   _____

3. What do you consider your greatest accomplishment? Why?

   _____

   _____

   _____

4. What would your best friend say is your most positive attribute? Why?

   _____

   _____

   _____

5. What was the most positive message your parents gave you? Why?

    _____

    _____

    _____

6. What would you most like to be remembered for in your life? Why?

    _____

    _____

    _____

7. Circle the words that you believe *best* describe your character, talents, and appearance.

Talented	Motivated	Humorous	Outgoing
Creative	Responsible	Organized	Reserved
Caring	Professional	Understanding	Athletic
Mature	Technical	Attractive	A leader

8. List briefly, what you are most proud of:

- A difficult job. _____

- A goal you reached. _____

- An award you received. _____

- A compliment you gave. _____

- A compliment you received. _____

- A habit you changed. _____

EXERCISE 2.3   ASSESSING YOUR SOCIAL DECENTERING SKILL

Purposes:
1.   To better understand the way people socially decenter
2.   To increase your awareness of your own social decentering skill
3.   To consider the impact of social decentering on interpersonal communication

Directions:
Write a number in front of each item using the scale below to indicate how much each statement describes you and your experiences.

1--------------------2---------------------3---------------------4--------------------5
Strongly Disagree Disagree   Agree/Disagree   Agree   Strongly Agree

1 _____ I get emotional over almost anybody's crisis.

2 _____ I have wondered what people in some foreign countries think about various world problems.

3 _____ I feel the pain my closest friends feel when they are in trouble.

4 _____ I would feel some of the same feelings as a close friend (think of a particular friend) if both his/her parents were killed in an automobile accident; my friend would probably have some feelings I would not feel, as well.

5 _____ I would feel some of the feelings that a senior citizen I was talking to might have upon learning of the death of their spouse of fifty years.

6 _____ I think about how I would handle situations confronting other people that I hear or read about.

7 _____ When I hear about a person's problem that is similar to a problem I've experienced, I usually recall what I thought and did about my problem.

8 _____ I get emotionally involved in news stories about the tragedies and joys of other people.

9 _____ I take into consideration both the situation and a person's cultural and ethnic background when I'm trying to understand the behavior of someone I don't know very well.

10 ____ My emotions are easily aroused when I am imagining myself in another person's predicament.

11 ____ (Think of a particular friendship that you have recently developed). I have tried to understand how this person thinks by considering their background, personality, maturity, etc.

12 ____ I sometimes think about how my closest friend will think about a controversial subject even before we start to discuss it.

Process Types:

Use of Your Self	Total items: 1, 6, 7, & 10	_____
Use of the Specific Other:	Total items: 3, 4, 11, & 12	_____
Use of a Generalized Other:	Total items: 2, 5, 8, & 9	_____

Overall Social Decentering Score: Total of all items: _____

Questions:

1. Use of Self involves thinking about your own experiences and applying them to others. Use of the Specific Other involves thinking about what you know or observe about specific people while considering what is occurring to them. Use of a Generalized Other is the application of your general views about various groups of people to individuals whom you identify as being members of those groups. For which of the three processes did you have the highest score? The lowest? Why do you think that is?

2. What could you do to increase you ability in the process for which you received the lowest score?

3. The midpoint for the overall social decentering scores is 32.5 which means that a score of less than 27 indicates less tendency to socially decenter, while a score of 38 or above indicates greater tendency to socially decenter. What does your score indicate about your social decentering skill? How well does the score reflect your own impression of how well you take on other people's perspectives? Why?

4. Are their some circumstances in which you effectively socially decenter? If so, what were they?

5. What are some of the situations in which you failed to effectively socially decenter? What was the impact on the interaction? On the relationship?

EXERCISE 2.4   INTERPERSONAL NEEDS

Purpose:
1. To better understand Schutz' theory of three interpersonal needs.
2. To determine your own level of interpersonal needs.
3. To examine how your interpersonal needs affect your interpersonal relationships.

Directions:
For each of the described interpersonal needs, record your self-rating in the column labeled "Self" using a scale from 1 (low) to 5 (high). Have a friend or classmate provide his or her self-ratings in the "Other" column.

Interpersonal Needs	Descriptions	Self	Other

Expressed Inclusion: *Interest*. Desire to include others in what you do. **High:** Comfortable with others; need others around to enjoy things. **Low:** Comfortable alone; engages in individual activity.

Wanted Inclusion: *Acceptance*. Desire to have others include you. **High:** Not selective about who you do things with. Wants to be invited to join others. **Low:** Selective about whom you do things with Works alone. Doesn't mind not being included.

Expressed Control: *Leadership*. Amount of decision making responsibility you want. **High:** Likes to control situations. Likes to make decisions for yourself and others. **Low:** Avoids decision making. Avoids responsibility.

Wanted Control: *Guidance*. Comfort with others making decisions for you. Confidence/respect for others. **High:** Likes others to make decisions. Respects other's ability to decide. **Low:** Low respect for other's decision making.

Expressed Affection: *Liking others*. Involvement with others. Sharing of emotions. **High:** Readily accepts emotional involvement. Helps others feel nurtured. Strong relationship initiator. **Low:** Cautious in sharing emotions. Tends not to initiate relationships.

Wanted Affection: *Closeness*. Desire for affection; comfort in approaching others. **High:** Wants a great deal of affection. Comfortable being approached. **Low:** Uncomfortable when other people approach. Uncomfortable with affection from others.

<u>Questions</u>

1. What are your areas of greatest interpersonal needs? Least?

2. How do your various needs affect your interactions with other people?

3. Which needs are most compatible between you and the other person? (for control this is usually when one person is high and the other person is low) Which are least?

4. How is your communication affected or likely to be affected by the need similarities and differences between you and your partner?

EXERCISE 2.5　　WEARING MANY HATS

Purposes:
1.　To realize some of the different roles you perform in one day.
2.　To become aware of how roles affect behavior and communication.
3.　To understand the influence of gender on roles you perform.

Directions:
1.　List three roles you performed last week (for example: student, friend, brother/sister, cashier, food service worker, club secretary, basketball player, and boyfriend/girlfriend).
2.　Identify the expected behaviors, especially communication behaviors, for you in each of your roles (behaviors expected).
3.　Analyze how your expectations developed (origins of expectations).

1. Role: _____

Behaviors Expected _____

_____

Origins of expectations: _____

_____

2. Role: _____

Behaviors Expected _____

_____

Origins of expectations: _____

_____

3. Role: _____

Behaviors Expected _____

_____

Origins of expectations: _____

_____

Questions:
1.　Which role is easiest for you to enact? Which most difficult? Why?

2.　In what ways are the behaviors dictated by social sex roles (gender stereotypes)?

3.　How do these gender stereotypical role expectations affect your interactions with others?

EXERCISE 2.6   DISCOVERING IMPACTS ON YOUR SELF-ESTEEM

Purposes:
1. To understand who and/or what influences the positive and negative views you have about yourself.
2. To realize the ways others influence your self and why.

Directions:

POSITIVE IMPACT

1. List three people, events, accomplishments, etc. that make a positive impact on your self-concept.
2. State what each of these people do or what happened during an event to make the positive impact.

	WHAT/WHO	HOW/WHY
1.		
2.		
3.		

How you can INCREASE OR MAINTAIN the positive impact:

_____

NEGATIVE IMPACT

1. List three people, events, accomplishments, etc. that make a negative impact on your self-concept.
2. State what each of these people do or what happened during an event to make the negative impact.

	WHO/WHAT	HOW/WHY
1.		
2.		
3.		

How you can DECREASE the negative impact:

_____

EXERCISE 2.7 CHANGING NEGATIVE MESSAGES INTO POSITIVE

Purpose:
1. To learn to turn negative messages about our selves into positive messages.

Directions:
1. List five negative messages about your "self" that you either remember receiving as a child or messages that you've heard recently. For example, "You are just a pesky, tagalong brat" or "You're too possessive; I think we need to break up."

_____

1.

2.

3.

4.

5.

Now turn these same five negative messages into positive ones by putting the statement in the first person (I or my), using the present tense, and/or stating what you want. Example: "I learned valuable lessons by being with my brother/sister."

1.

2.

3.

4.

5.

Put all five of your positive statements on 3x5 cards and keep in a place you can see them daily. Any time you hear a negative message, turn it into a positive message in the same way and put it on a 3x5 card to add to your collection of positive self-esteem builders.

EXERCISE 2.8　　　CHOOSING TO AVOID DISCLOSURE

Purpose:
1. To identify reasons you do not disclose information to other people.
2. Understanding communication privacy management theory.

Directions:
1. Choose a particular person with whom you want to analyze your self-disclosing behavior (a close friend, a family member, a co-worker, etc.).
2. In the column on the left of each item below, indicate the extent to which you use each reason to avoid disclosing:
   5 = Almost always　　4 = Often　　3 = Sometimes　　2 = Rarely　　1 = Never

_____　　1.　I can't find the opportunity to self-disclose with this person.

_____　　2.　If I disclose, I might hurt the other person.

_____　　3.　If I disclose, the other person might evaluate or judge me.

_____　　4.　I can't think of topics that I would disclose.

_____　　5.　Self-disclosure would give information that might be used against me at sometime.

_____　　6.　I don't believe in self-disclosing until the relationship is very close.

_____　　7.　Self-disclosure might threaten relationships I have with people other than the close acquaintance to whom I disclose.

_____　　8.　Self-disclosure is a sign of weakness.

_____　　9.　If I disclose, I might lose control to the other person.

_____　　10.　I don't like other people knowing very much about me.

_____　　11.　If I disclose, I might project an image I do not want to project.

_____　　12.　My disclosures might be misunderstood.

_____　　13.　If I disclose, the other person might evaluate me negatively.

_____　　14.　Self-disclosure is a sign of some emotional weakness.

_____ 15. Self-disclosure might hurt our relationship.

_____ 16. I am afraid that self-disclosure might give the other person the impression that I want a more intimate relationship than I really do.

_____ 17. Self-disclosure might threaten my physical safety.

_____ 18. If I disclose, I might give information that makes me appear inconsistent.

_____ 19. I was taught not to reveal information about myself.

_____ 20. Any other reasons: _____

Questions:

1. Which reasons do you use most often to avoid disclosing to this person?

2. Are the reasons you use most often realistic or legitimate reasons to avoid sharing information with this person? Why?

3. To what degree are your patterns of disclosure (creation of boundaries) due to:
    A. your cultural background

    B. your need to connect or not connect with others

    C. the amount of risk (embarrassment) involved in sharing information

EXERCISE 2.9   DIAGRAMMING SOCIAL PENETRATION

Purpose:
1. To help you understand the breadth and depth of self-disclosure.
2. To help you see the differences in the breadth and depth of self-disclosure between types of relationships.

Directions:
1. Use the following forms to make social penetration models for four different relationships: (A.) A close same-sex friend, (B.) A close opposite-sex friend, (C.) A parent or other close relative, and (D.) A work place relationship.
2. Fill in the pies to indicate the depth of your disclosures for each of the twelve issues listed by number as they correspond to each diagram. The more toward the center of the pie you shade in, the more intimate your disclosures.

TWELVE QUALITIES ABOUT YOURSELF:

1. Religious views.
2. Political views.
3. Activities.
4. Education.
5. Family.
6. Your upbringing.
7. Sexual issues.
8. Job experiences/career plans.
9. Personality.
10. Health and medical history.
11. Skills possessed and desired.
12. Weaknesses and faults.

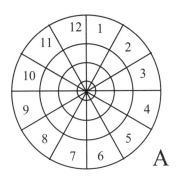
A

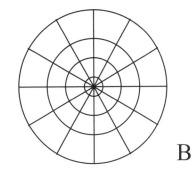
B

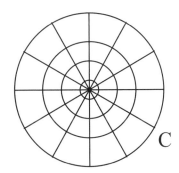
C

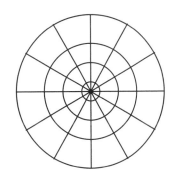
D

Questions:

1. How deep or shallow are your relationships with these people?

2. Are you satisfied with the depth and breadth of these relationships?

3. What could you do to change any of these relationships?

4. What inferences could a person make about each relationship by looking at the diagram (you could ask a classmate to describe how they see each of your diagrams)?

5. What changes have occurred in your diagrams in the last month?

6. What changes have occurred in your diagrams in the last six months?

EXERCISE 2.10   SOCIAL PENETRATION AND SELECTIVE SELF-DISCLOSURES

Purposes:
1. To illustrate how we disclose different things to different people.
2. To understand how different people might have different images of who we are.
3. To understand how social penetration leads to differing levels of intimacy.

Directions:
1. Fill in ten pieces of information about yourself down the left hand side of the page according to how much risk you feel in disclosing such information. Start with the qualities that you are most comfortable having people know and end with those that you are least comfortable having people know.
2. Put the first names of people described in the blanks below the descriptions.
3. Put a check after each quality about yourself that is known by the other person.

	Best Friend Same Sex	Casual Friend Opposite Sex	Casual Friend Same Sex	Parent
NAMES =	_____	_____	_____	_____
Self-Information				
1. _____				
_____	_____	_____	_____	_____
2. _____				
_____	_____	_____	_____	_____
3. _____				
_____	_____	_____	_____	_____
4. _____				
_____	_____	_____	_____	_____
5. _____				
_____	_____	_____	_____	_____
6. _____				
_____	_____	_____	_____	_____
7. _____				
_____	_____	_____	_____	_____
8. _____				
_____	_____	_____	_____	_____

9. _____

_____ _____ _____ _____ _____

10 _____

_____ _____ _____ _____ _____

<u>Questions:</u>

1. With whom do you share the **<u>most</u>** information? Why?

2. With whom do you share the **<u>least</u>** amount of information? Why?

3. What information is most difficult for you to share with other people?

4. In what ways do the types of information you disclose define the nature of your relationships?

5. To what degree does the number of checks you have reflect how open or closed you are in disclosing yourself to other people?

6. What disclosures are affected by the sex of the other person?

EXERCISE 2.11   MAKING A JOHARI WINDOW

Purposes:
1. To see how the Johari Window can be used to represent relationships.
2. To see how the amount of self-disclosure defines relationships.

Directions:
1. Review the material in the text on the four quadrants that make up the Johari Window. The open quadrant is how much information about you that your partner knows, the blind quadrant is information your partner knows about you that you don't know about yourself, the hidden quadrant is information you know about yourself that your partner doesn't know, and the unknown quadrant is information about yourself that neither you or your partner knows yet.

2. A. Draw a window that shows the relationship you have with a close friend of the opposite sex.

    B. Draw a window that shows the relationship you have with a close friend of the same sex.

3. A. Draw a window that shows your relationship with a casual friend of the opposite sex.

    B. Draw a window that shows your relationship with a casual friend of the same sex.

4. A. Draw a window that shows your relationship with your mother or other close female relative.

B. Draw a window that shows your relationship with your father or other close male relative.

Questions:

1. What quadrants tend to vary the most from relationship to relationship?

2. What gender differences, if any, are there in your windows?

3. What window has changed the most over the last year? In what ways has it changed?

4. How are the windows likely to change in the future?

**EXERCISE 2.12   SELF-DISCLOSURE ACROSS THE LIFE OF A
                    RELATIONSHIP**

Purpose:
1.   To see how self-disclosure occurs over the life span of relationships.

Directions:
1.   Think of three close relationships you have; one that has existed a long time, one that
     is fairly recent, and one with someone who was an acquaintance for a long time first
     before you became close.
2.   Draw a graph for each relationship that plots the "amount" of self-disclosure that
     occurred at any given moment of time against a time line of how long you have
     known each person.

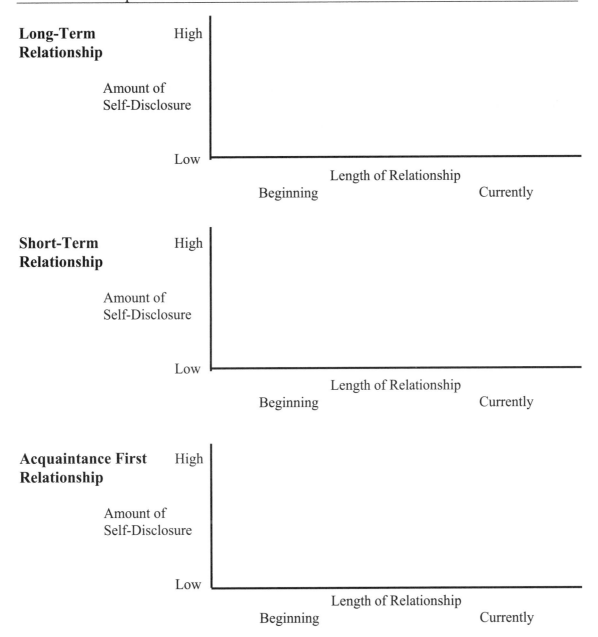

Questions:

1. What do you notice is different between the self-disclosure patterns for the three relationships?

2. What do you notice is the same between the self-disclosure patterns for the three relationships?

3. Plot a dotted line on each of the three that reflects how the "depth" or level of intimacy has changed in your self-disclosures over the same period of time. How do these compare across the three relationships?

4. How does the amount of self-disclosure relate to the depth of disclosures in each of your three relationships? What does that tell about the three relationships?

5. What conclusions or inferences can you draw about your own patterns of self-disclosure in relationships?

EXERCISE 2.13   A SELF STUDY OF SELF-DISCLOSURE GUIDELINES

Purpose:
1. To reflect on the guidelines you follow when self-disclosing to other people.

Directions:
1. Before proceeding with this exercise you need to have engaged in a personal conversation with either a stranger or an acquaintance for at least ten minutes. If you haven't, then seek out an opportunity to do so before proceeding with the questions listed below.
2. Each question reflects information in the text on guidelines for self-disclosing. Consider the guidelines inherent in each question and assess your tendency to follow or violate those guidelines and the impact on relationship development.

Questions:
1. What information did you disclose because you thought the other would find it interesting and be comfortable hearing it?

2. What information did you NOT disclose because you thought the other would not find it interesting or would be uncomfortable hearing it?

3. What do your responses to questions 1 and 2 suggest about your being other-centered?

4. Were you aware of the other person's nonverbal responses to your self-disclosing? If so, what nonverbal cues did the other person display that reflected either interest and comfort in hearing your self-disclosures or lack of interest/discomfort?

5. How would you rate your level of disclosure: too little, too much, or just right? How can you tell?

6. What was the most personal piece of information you revealed about yourself? To what degree was this revelation appropriate or inappropriate? How can you tell?

EXERCISE 2.14   **A STUDY OF OTHER PEOPLE'S USE OF**
                                   SELF-DISCLOSURE GUIDELINES

Purpose:

1. To observe and reflect on other people's use of self-disclosure guidelines.

Directions:

1. Review the list of questions below associated with other people's use of self-disclosure guidelines before proceeding.
2. Put yourself in a situation where you can consciously attend to the manner in which a stranger or acquaintance interacts with you. After that interaction, return to this set of questions and record your responses.
3. Each question reflects information in the text on guidelines for self-disclosing. Consider the guidelines inherent in each question and assess your tendency to follow or violate those guidelines and the impact on relationship development.

Questions:

1. What information did the other person disclose that you found interesting and comfortable hearing?

2. What information did the other person disclose that you found uninteresting or were uncomfortable hearing?

3A. What verbal and nonverbal expressions did you communicate (if any) to indicate support, attentiveness, and responsiveness to the other person's self-disclosures?

3B. How did the other person respond to these expressions or lack thereof?

4. How would you rate the other person's level of disclosure: too little, too much, or just right? How did that level make you feel?

5. What was the most personal piece of information the other person revealed to you? To what degree did you feel this revelation appropriate or inappropriate? How did you react?

6. Overall, did the other person appear comfortable or uncomfortable self-disclosing to you? What did you do that either fostered or inhibited his or her self-disclosing?

Self	Self Concept
Attitude	Belief
Value	Material Self
Social Self	Spiritual Self
Looking Glass Self	Androgynous Role
Self-reflexiveness	Self-worth (Self-esteem)

Person's subjective description of who he or she is.	Sum total of who a person is; a person's central inner force.
Ways in which you structure your understanding of reality-what is true and what is false for you.	Learned predisposition to respond to a person, object, or idea in a favorable or unfavorable way.
Concept of self as reflected in a total of all of the tangible things you own.	Enduring concept of good and bad, right and wrong.
Concept of self based on your thoughts and introspection about personal values, moral standards, and beliefs.	Concept of self as reflected in your personal, social interactions with others.
Gender role that includes both masculine and feminine qualities.	Concept that suggests you learn who you are based upon your interactions with others, who reflect your self back to you.
Your evaluation of your worth or value based on your perception of such things as your skills, abilities, talents, and appearance.	Ability to think about what you are doing while you are doing it.

Subjective Self-Awareness	Objective Self-Awareness
Symbolic Self-Awareness	Symbolic Interaction Theory
Life Position	Specific-Other Perspective
Generalized-Other Perspective	Self-Fulfilling Prophesy
Social Support	Intrapersonal Communication
Talk Therapy	Reframing

Ability to be the object of one's own thoughts and attention—to be aware of one's state of mind and that one is thinking.	Ability to differentiate the self from the social and physical environment.
Theory that people make sense of the world on the basis of their interactions with other people.	Uniquely human ability to think about oneself and use language (symbols) to represent oneself to others.
Perspective that uses information that one can observe or imagine about another person to predict that person's behavior.	Feelings of regard for yourself and others, as reflected in your sense of worth and self-esteem.
Prediction about your future actions that is likely to come true because you believe it will come true.	Perspective that uses observed or imagined information about many people, or people in general, to predict a person's behavior.
Communication within yourself; self talk	Expression of empathy and concern for others that is communicated while listening to them and offering positive and encouraging words.
Process of redefining events and experience from a different point of view	Technique in which a person describes his or her problems and concerns to a skilled listener in order to better understand the emotions and issues that are creating the problems.

Visualization	Need for control
Need for Inclusion	Social Comparison
Need for Affection	Psychology
Social Decentering	Communibiological Approach
Personality	Communication Apprehension
Shyness	Communication Style

Interpersonal need for some degree of domination in our relationships as well as the need to be controlled.	Technique of imagining that you are performing a particular task in a certain way; positive visualization can enhance self-esteem.
Process of comparing yourself to others who are similar to you to measure your worth and value.	Interpersonal need to be included and to include others in social activities
Study of how thinking influences behavior.	Interpersonal need to give and receive love, personal support, warmth, and intimacy.
Perspective that suggests that genetics and biological influences play a major role in influencing our communication behavior.	Cognitive process in which you take into account another person's thoughts, feelings, values, background, and perspective.
Fear or anxiety associated with either real or anticipated communication with other people.	Set of enduring internal predispositions and behavioral characteristics that describe how people react to their environment.
Style that is identifiable by habitual way in which you communicate with other people.	Tendency to not talk or interact with other people

Willingness to Communicate	Assertiveness
Responsiveness	Self Disclosure
Self Awareness	Johari Window Model
Social Penetration Model	Dyadic Effect
Symbolic Interaction Theory	Psychology
Facework	Face

Tendency to make requests, ask for information, and generally pursue your own rights and best interests.	General characteristic, which describes an individual's tendencies to be shy or apprehensive about communicating with other people.
Purposefully providing information about yourself to others that they would not learn if you did not tell them.	Tendency to be sensitive to the needs of others, including being sympathetic to others' feelings and placing the feelings of others above your own feelings.
Model of self-disclosure that summarizes how self awareness is influenced by self-disclosure and information about yourself from others.	Person's conscious understanding of who he or she is.
The reciprocal nature of self-disclosure: "You disclose to me, and I'll disclose to you."	Model of self-disclosure and relational development that reflects both depth and breadth of shared information.
The study of how thinking influences behavior.	The theory that people make sense of the world on the basis of their interactions with other people
Person's positive perception of himself or herself in interactions with others.	Using communication to maintain your own positive self-perception (self-face) or to support, reinforce, or challenge someone else's self-perception (other-face).

Willingness to Communicate	Communication Privacy Management Theory

Theory that suggest that we each manage our own degree of privacy by means of personal boundaries and rules for sharing information.	General term for the likelihood that an individual will communicate with others in certain situations.

CHAPTER 3
INTERPERSONAL COMMUNICATION AND PERCEPTION

OBJECTIVES

After studying the material in this chapter of *Interpersonal Communication: Relating to Others* and completing the exercises in this section of the study guide, you should understand:

1. The definitions of perception and interpersonal perception.
2. The three stages of interpersonal perception.
3. How interpersonal perception is related to interpersonal communication.
4. The processes of how we form impressions of other people, describe other people, and interpret other people's behaviors.
5. The eight factors which distort the accuracy of our interpersonal perceptions.
6. The five suggestions on how to improve you interpersonal perceptions.

STUDY QUESTIONS

You should be able to answer the following questions:

1. What is the definition of perception and interpersonal perception?
2. What are the three stages of interpersonal perception and what happens in each stage?
3. What is meant by selective perception, selective attention, selective exposure, and selective recall?
4. What is the difference between passive perception and active perception?
5. How do the primacy effect and the recency effect relate to impression formation?
6. How does the implicit personality theory relate to interpersonal perception?
7. What is meant by the halo effect and horn effect?
8. What is attribution theory?
9. How does standpoint theory explain perceptual differences?
10. What are the barriers to making accurate perceptions?
11. How can you improve your ability to make accurate interpersonal perceptions?

EXERCISE 3.1   CATEGORIZING OTHERS BY LIKES AND DISLIKES

Purpose:
1. To become aware of how you perceive people differently because of your attraction level to them.

Directions:
1. Make a list of three people that you like.
2. Write down as many personal characteristics and qualities as you can think of about each person.
3. Make a list of three people that you don't like.
4. Write down as many personal characteristics and qualities as you can think of about each person.

PEOPLE YOU LIKE   **CHARACTERISTICS**

1. _____   _____

                             _____

                             _____

                             _____

2. _____   _____

                             _____

                             _____

                             _____

3. _____   _____

                             _____

                             _____

                             _____

PEOPLE YOU DON'T LIKE   **CHARACTERISTICS**

1. _____   _____

   _____

   _____

   _____

2. _____   _____

   _____

   _____

   _____

3. _____   _____

   _____

   _____

   _____

Questions:

1. When comparing the lists, what positive (complimentary) characteristics did you have? _____

   _____

2. Which list had the most positive characteristics? Why do you think that happened?

   _____

   _____

3. What negative (uncomplimentary) characteristics did you observe?

   _____

   _____

4. Which had the most negative qualities? Why do you think that happened?

   _____

   _____

EXERCISE 3.2   INTERPERSONAL PERCEPTION: CATEGORIES

Purposes:
1. To understand the use of categories as part of organizing perception.
2. To identify categories (constructs) you apply to your perceptions of people.

Directions:
1. We often classify people according to a set of bipolar terms (constructs) such as: active-passive, outgoing-shy, warm-cold, masculine-feminine. Think about the way you classify the people you meet and know. Write down one of the bipolar terms/categories that best reflect the classifications you use in Column A and its counterpart in Column C.

	Column A	Column B	Column C	Column D
a.	_____	_____	_____	_____
b.	_____	_____	_____	_____
c.	_____	_____	_____	_____
d.	_____	_____	_____	_____
e.	_____	_____	_____	_____
f.	_____	_____	_____	_____
g.	_____	_____	_____	_____
h.	_____	_____	_____	_____

2.   In columns B and D, write the names of people you know that fit that category.

Questions:
1. How easy was it for you to identify the categories you use? What does this say about your perceptual organizing skills?

2. How easy was it to identify people that fit your categories? What does this say about the legitimacy of the categories (do you really use them)?

3. What categories do you use the most? Least? Why?

4. How might your categories affect your interpersonal communication?

EXERCISE 3.3   INTERPERSONAL PERCEPTION: STAGES

Purposes:
1. To understand the three stages of interpersonal perception.
2. To identify basic perceptual biases.

Directions:
1. Record your impressions or interpretations of each of the five drawings in the lines listed under each drawing.

2. Be sure to do step 1 before looking at the questions below.

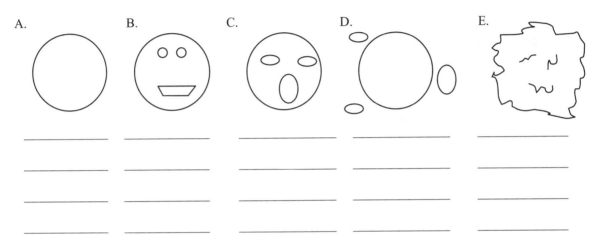

A.   B.   C.   D.   E.

_____   _____   _____   _____   _____

_____   _____   _____   _____   _____

_____   _____   _____   _____   _____

_____   _____   _____   _____   _____

Questions:
1. In what ways has the organization of the elements making up each drawing affected your impression? For example; drawings C and D are made up of the same four elements, but did you have the same impression for each?

2. In what ways have you "superimposed" your experiences onto the five figures to make sense of them? (Hint: these are really just circles and lines).

3. Compare your list of words with classmates or ask friends for their reactions. For which figures was there the most agreement? Disagreement? Why?

EXERCISE 3.4   SELECTIVE PERCEPTION, ATTENTION, EXPOSURE, RECALL

Purposes:
1. To understand the principles of selectivity.
2. To become aware of your own perceptual selectivity.

Directions:
1. One problem in becoming aware of your selectivity it that is occurring without you even realizing you are doing it; so for this exercise you need to be objective, honest, and highly introspective.
2. Follow the instructions provided for each type of selectivity.

Selective Perception: (seeing and hearing what you want; filtering out what you don't).
  1. List two occasions where others have pointed out your failure to recognize something because of your selective perception (For example, didn't notice a negative quality in someone you were attracted to, or not hearing instructions on how long an assignment was supposed to be)

  2. What personal factors affective these perceptions (beliefs, attitudes, hopes, fears, culture, etc.):

Selective Attention: (attention affected by your needs or qualities in the stimulus).
  1. List two recent situations where you directed your attention because of some need (focusing only on restaurants while driving because you were hungry)

  2. To what degree did you miss noticing other things or were oblivious to other things because your attention was focused by your needs.

  3. List two recent situations where something caught your eye or ear.

  4. What was it about the items that caught your attention?

Selective Exposure: (seeking out reinforcement of existing beliefs, values, etc.)

1. List two situations where you attended or participated in something because it reinforced your existing attitudes, beliefs, values and behaviors (for example, attending or watching a speech on TV in support of something you believe in or reading an article online that supports a particular attitude you hold).

2. What are the advantages of these selective exposures?

3. What are the disadvantages of these selective exposures?

Selective Recall: (only remembering what we want; avoiding unpleasant memories).

1. List two positive memories from two generally unpleasant situations (for example, remembering a fun time you had with someone you eventually came to dislike or recalling a pleasant relationship at a workplace you came to despise).

2. List two occasions where a discussion with a family member or friend reminded you of a memory that you had forgotten or chosen not to recall.

3. In what ways has your selective recall be an advantage? A disadvantage?

EXERCISE 3.5   EVERYONE'S A CRITIC (PERCEPTION of MOVIES)

Purposes:
1. To understand Standpoint Theory by applying it to how different people see the same thing differently.
2. To explore how our perception is affected by various factors.

Directions:
1. Think about a recent movie that you have seen and answer the questions about the movie in the space provided.
2. Find someone else who has seen the movie but with whom you have not previously discussed it. Ask them the questions and fill in his or her responses. Now find a second person and fill them out again.

a. <u>Did you like the movie? Why or why not?</u>
Your Answer:

Friend # 1's Answer

Friend # 2's Answer

b. <u>What character(s) did you like the most? Why?</u>
Your Answer:

Friend # 1's Answer

Friend # 2's Answer

c. <u>What character(s) did you like the least? Why?</u>
Your Answer:

Friend # 1's Answer

Friend # 2's Answer

d. <u>Describe the basic premise of the movie.</u>
Your Answer:

Friend # 1's Answer

Friend # 2's Answer

e. <u>What was your favorite part of the movie?</u> (If you didn't like the movie, try to answer with more than just "the end"). <u>Why was it your favorite?</u>
Your Answer:

Friend # 1's Answer

Friend # 2's Answer

Questions:

1. In what ways were your perceptions the same as the two other people? How is it that all three of you had the same reaction?

2. In what ways were your perceptions different from the other two people? What made them different?

3. What aspects of your social position, power or cultural background affected your perceptions differently than the other two people? What aspects of their social position, power, or cultural background affected their perceptions?

4. Did the other two people say anything that changed the way you perceived the movie? Have you ever changed your view of a movie after talking about the movie with other people?

EXERCISE 3.6   EXPLAINING WHY PEOPLE DO WHAT THEY DO

Purposes:
1.   To understand the interpretations you make about others' behavior.
2.   To apply attribution theory by explaining behavior through intentionality, circumstance, stimulus, and person.

Directions:
1.   For the next few days, observe three people engaging in some strange, unusual, or unpredictable manner and record your interpretations of their behavior.
2.   After recording the information, explain possible intentionality or unintentionality of the behavior (Did they do the behavior on purpose?).
3.   Explain the possible causes for the each person's behavior due to circumstance, stimulus, and person.

PERSON #1
Describe behavior: _____

_____

Give a possible intentional explanation for the behavior: _____

_____

Give a possible unintentional explanation for the behavior: _____

_____

State a possible circumstantial (external) cause for the behavior: _____

_____

State a possible stimulus (external) cause for the behavior: _____

_____

State a possible person (internal) cause for the behavior: _____

_____

PERSON #2
Describe behavior: _____

_____

Give a possible intentional explanation for the behavior: _____

_____

Give a possible unintentional explanation for the behavior: _____

_____

State a possible circumstantial cause (external) for the behavior: _____

_____

State a possible stimulus (external) cause for the behavior: _____

_____

State a possible person (internal) cause for the behavior: _____

_____

PERSON #3
Describe behavior: _____

_____

Give a possible intentional explanation for the behavior: _____

_____

Give a possible unintentional explanation for the behavior: _____

_____

State a possible circumstantial cause (external) for the behavior: _____

_____

State a possible stimulus (external) cause for the behavior: _____

_____

State a possible person (internal) cause for the behavior: _____

_____

Questions:

1. Which cause for behavior (circumstance, stimulus, or person) was the easiest to generate? Why might that be?

2. For each of the three people, which attribution of cause do you feel is most likely? Why?

3. How confident to you feel that your explanation for each of the three behaviors is accurate? What contributes to or diminishes your level of confidence?

4. To what degree does your familiarity with the particular behavior or person affect the attribution of cause and interpretation of the behaviors?

EXERCISE 3.7   DIFFERENCES IN PERCEPTION

Purposes:
1.   To demonstrate personal qualities can be viewed differently by different people.
2.   To demonstrate the creation of constructs to describe ourselves.

Directions:
1.   In the space below write a list of five qualities about yourself (these are personal constructs).
2.   In the space provided write down a negative synonym for each quality. These could be the way someone else perceives your quality.

	Example: Personal Quality:		Negative Synonym
	Frugal	→	Cheap
	Conservative	→	Red-neck
	Fun loving	→	Lacks goals

Personal Quality   **Negative Synonyms**

   1.   1.

   2.   2.

   3.   3.

   4.   4.

   5.   5.

Questions:
1.   What examples can you think of in your life where someone else has viewed a quality about yourself differently than you?

2.   What impact did these differences have on your relationship?

3.   What negative perceptions of other people's qualities do you have that could be described in a more positive manner?

EXERCISE 3.8   CREATING A PERCEPTION JOURNAL

Purpose:
1. To realize the impact that perceptions have on communication behavior.

Directions:
1. Over the next few days, observe the interpersonal interactions that you have with four different individuals.
2. Record your observations of the behavior of each person.
3. Give your interpretation or attribution of meaning to each of the behaviors.
4. Explain how your interpretation affected your behavior toward the other person.
5. After the interaction has ended, ask the other person to explain their behavior or to explain what meaning they intended by their behavior.

OBSERVATION	INTERPRETATION	AFFECT ON MY BEHAVIOR	OTHER'S EXPLANATION
My roommate came in, slamming things around the room, swearing, and scowling.	*My roommate was angry at me for leaving stuff on the floor.*	*I got mad and started to call my roommate names and walked out of the place.*	*When I came back, I asked my roommate why he/she was angry. It was because he/she just flunked a test and he/she was worried about staying on the Dean's List.*

1.

2.

OBSERVATION	INTERPRETATION	AFFECT ON MY BEHAVIOR	OTHER'S EXPLANATION
3.			
4.			

Questions:

1. Which perceptions were most correct?

2. What is your relationship to the person(s) that you were able to accurately perceive their behavior? Why do you think relationship contributed to your accuracy?

3. What is your relationship to the person(s) that you had the most difficulty making accurate perceptions of behavior? Why do you think relationship contributed to your inaccuracy?

EXERCISE 3.9 ASSESSING YOUR PERCEPTUAL BIASES

Purposes:
1. To understand the major barriers to accurate interpersonal perception.
2. To examine your own perceptual biases.

Directions:
1. For each perceptual barrier listed below, see if you can think of a recent example where the barrier affected your perceptions of other people. Write down any impact it might have had on your interpersonal communication or the relationship.

Ignoring Information (not focusing on important information).

Over generalizing (treating a small piece of information as highly representative)

Oversimplify (preferring a simple explanation to a complex one)

Stereotyping (using preexisting rigid expectation about another person)

Imposing Consistency (seeing another person's behavior as more consistent than it is)

Focusing on the Negative (giving more weight to negative information than positive)

Blaming Others by Assuming They Have Control (fundamental attribution error)

Avoiding Responsibility (others cause our problems; our skills produce our successes)

Questions:

1. For which of the barriers did an example come most readily to mind? How representative are these examples of recurring barriers you experience?

2. For which of the barriers did you have the hardest time identifying an example? Discuss whether this is because it doesn't happen much or because you are less aware of it happening.

3. What can you do to minimize the impact of these barriers on future perceptions?

EXERCISE 3.10   CHECKING YOUR PERCEPTIONS

Purpose:
1. To practice checking on the accuracy of your perceptions in your interpersonal interactions.

Directions:
1. In three different interpersonal interactions you have in the next few days, observe behaviors that confuse you or where the meaning of the behavior is not clear to you. Try to include at least one person from a different cultural background than yours.
2. Make an interpretation of each of the behaviors.
3. Practice using indirect perception checking to determine if your interpretation of the behavior is correct or not by paying closer attention to the other person's voice, words, and body movements.
4. To increase your accuracy, practice using direct perception checking by telling the other person what behaviors you are observing, what the behaviors mean to you, and then asking for confirmation of your interpretation.
5. Record a brief description of the interactions below, explaining the behaviors, your interpretations, what you focused on indirectly, and how you asked for confirmation directly.

PERSON #1

Description of the interaction: _____

Explanation of the behavior: _____

_____

Your meaning: _____

_____

What you focused on indirectly: _____

_____

How you checked your accuracy: _____

_____

PERSON #2

Description of the interaction:_____

Explanation of the behavior: _____

_____

Your meaning: _____

_____

What you focused on indirectly: _____

_____

How you checked your accuracy: _____

_____

PERSON #3

Description of the interaction:_____

Explanation of the behavior: _____

_____

Your meaning: _____

_____

What you focused on indirectly: _____

_____

How you checked your accuracy: _____

_____

Questions:

1.   In which situations were your perceptions most accurate?

_____

_____

2.   What information helped you make perceptions most accurately?_____

_____

_____

EXERCISE 3.11   FOCUSING ON THE OBVIOUS

Purposes:
1. To become aware of the type of information you take in when meeting new people.
2. To understand how you structure information by categories such as physical, role, psychological, and social behavior.
3. To identify perceptual barriers that might affect our impressions of others.

Directions:
1. Observe 10 strangers whom you encounter on campus, in town, or at a Mall.
2. Write down your first impression of each person.
3. List the information that led to your impression of each.

PERSON	IMPRESSION	INFORMATION USED
1.		
2.		
3.		
4.		
5.		
6.		

Person	Impression	Information Used
7.		
8.		
9.		
10.		

Questions:

1. A. What information did you use most frequently in forming your impressions?

_____

_____

_____

_____

B. To what degree does this reflect bias in your interpersonal perceptions?

_____

_____

_____

_____

2. A. What information was specific to only one individual?

_____

_____

_____

_____

B. How does this reflect on any bias in your interpersonal perceptions?

_____

_____

_____

_____

3.   What perceptual barriers are likely to have affected your impressions?

_____

_____

_____

_____

EXERCISE 3.12   MAKING POSITIVE AND NEGATIVE PERCEPTIONS

Purpose:
1.   To understand how judgments are made from different perspectives.

Directions:
1.   For each of the following situations, give a positive and a negative perception.

Situation #1: You see a "thirty-something" aged man leaning across a table and holding the hands of an older woman in a restaurant.

Positive:

Negative:

Situation # 2: You see a teenager giving money to a well-dressed man in the street.

Positive:

Negative:

Situation #3   You see the police pull up to your neighbor's house with all lights flashing.

Positive:

Negative:

Situation #4   You see a large, black dog standing over a screaming child lying on the ground.

Positive:

Negative:

Questions:

1.   Which perceptions were easiest to make--positive or negative? Why?

2.   What influenced your first reaction to each statement? Why?

3.   What does this exercise tell you about understanding a situation from the perspective of others?

Perception	Interpersonal Perception
Selective Perception	Punctuation
Selective Attention	Selective Exposure
Selective Recall	Thin Slicing
Closure	Superimpose
Passive Perception	Active Perception

Process of selecting, organizing, and interpreting your observations of other people.	Process of experiencing the world and making sense out of what you experience.
Process of making sense out of stimuli by grouping, dividing, organizing, separating, and categorizing information	Process of seeing, hearing, or making sense of the world around us based on such factors as our personality, beliefs, attitudes, hopes, fears, and culture, as well as what we like and don't like.
Tendency to put ourselves in situations that reinforce our attitudes, beliefs, values, or behaviors.	Process of focusing on specific stimuli, locking on to some things in the environment and ignoring others.
Observing a small sample of someone's behavior and then making a generalization about what the person is like, based on the sample.	Process that occurs when we remember things we want to remember and forget or repress things that are unpleasant, uncomfortable, or unimportant to us.
To place a familiar structure on information you select	Process of filling in missing information or gaps in what we perceive.
Perception that occurs because you seek out specific information through intentional observation and questioning.	Perception that occurs without conscious effort, but simply because your senses are in operation.

Impression	Impression Formation Theory
Primacy Effect	Recency Effect
Implicit Personality Theory	Halo Effect
Horn Effect	Construct
Standpoint Theory	Attribution Theory
Causal Attribution Theory	Stereotype

Theory that explains how you develop perceptions about people and how you maintain and use those perceptions to interpret their behaviors.	Collection of perceptions about others that you maintain and use to interpret their behaviors.
Tendency to attend to the most recent information observed about another person in order to form or modify an impression.	Tendency to attend to the first pieces of information you observed about another person in order to form an impression.
Attributing a variety of positive qualities to those you like.	Your unique set of beliefs and hypotheses about what people are like
Bipolar quality used to classify people.	Attributing a variety of negative qualities to those you dislike.
Theory that explains how you generate explanations for people's behaviors.	Theory that a person's social position, power, or cultural background influences how the person perceives the behavior of others.
To attribute a set of qualities to a person because of the person's membership in some category.	Theory of attribution that identifies the cause of a person's actions as circumstance, a stimulus, or the person himself or herself.

Indirect Perception Checking	Direct Perception Checking
Fundamental Attribution Error	Self-Serving Bias
Mindful	

Asking for confirmation from the observed person of an interpretation or a perception about him or her.	Seeking additional information to confirm or refute interpretations you are making through passive perception such as observing and listening
Tendency to perceive our own behavior as more positive than others' behavior.	Error that arises from attributing another person's behavior to internal, controllable causes, rather than to external, uncontrollable causes
	Conscious of what you are doing, thinking, and sensing at any given moment.

CHAPTER 4
INTERPERSONAL COMMUNICATION AND CULTURAL
DIVERSITY: ADAPTING TO OTHERS

OBJECTIVES

After studying the material in this chapter of *Interpersonal Communication: Relating to Others* and completing the exercises in this section of the study guide, you should understand:

1.   Differences in gender, sexual orientation, race and ethnicity, age, and social class as diversity.
2.   The meaning of culture and cultural diversity.
3.   The difference among cultural elements, values, and contexts.
4.   The difference between enculturation and acculturation.
5.   Hofstede's four cultural values.
6.   The difference between high-context and low-context cultures.
7.   The impact of ethnocentrism, different communication codes, stereotyping and prejudice, and assuming similarity, and assuming differences.
8.   The strategies for developing knowledge, motivation, and skills to effectively communicate in intercultural situations.
9.   The ways we can appropriately adapt to other people.

STUDY QUESTIONS

You should be able to answer the following questions:

1.   In what was are humans different/diverse?
2.   What is culture?
3.   How do cultural elements, values, goals, and contexts make up our cultural identity?
4.   What is the difference between enculturation and acculturation?
5.   What are the four variables that measure values in almost every culture?
6.   What is meant by masculine and feminine cultures?
7.   What is the difference between high-context and low context cultures and what countries are examples of each?
     What are the barriers to intercultural communication?
8.   What is ethnocentrism?
9.   How do cultural stereotypes and prejudice affect interpersonal communication?
10. What strategies can you use to help develop greater understanding between yourself and someone from a different culture?
11. How does social decentering and empathy impact intercultural communication?
12. How can you appropriately adapt your communication to others?

EXERCISE 4.1   DIVERSITY AND DIFFERENCES SELF-ASSESSMENT

Purpose:
1   To explore how differences affect interpersonal communication.
2.   To explore ways in which you are different from other people.

Directions:
1.   By this point in the term you should have some sense of the qualities possessed by your classmates (ages, hometowns, majors, etc.). Reflect on what qualities you possess that differ from the majority of your classmates as you respond to the assessment below.
2.   For each quality listed from the textbook answer the following:
"How does your quality affect your interactions with others who differ from you on that quality?" (for example, your gender affect interactions with the opposite sex?)

Gender

Sexual Orientation

Race

Ethnicity

Age

Social Class

3.   Besides those above, identify at least five qualities (can be physical, attitudes, values, beliefs, activities, interests, etc.) that you hold that are different from the majority of the other class members.
   a. _____
   b. _____
   c. _____
   d. _____
   e. _____

Questions:
1.   To what degree are you treated differently because of any of the above qualities?

2.   How do the above qualities affect the way you behave toward others?

EXERCISE 4.2   CULTURAL SELF-ASSESSMENT

Purpose:
1.   We often fail to recognize how our own lives are affected by the culture that surrounds us. This exercise identifies some aspects of your life that are affected by your culture.

Directions:
1.   Provide a response for each of the question below.
2.   The instructions often refer to parents and other family members. If those do not apply to you, answer those questions in terms of those who were most responsible for your upbringing.

Cultural Self Assessment

1.   Identify a specific and unique rule that your family follows at the dinner table:

2.   List a special activity, behavior, or tradition that occurs in your family during a specific holiday or for birthdays.

3.   How do the various members of your family greet each other? (How do you or other members of your family greet grandparents, parents, cousins, aunts, brothers, and sisters)?

4.   How does your family greet or treat visitors to your house?   Are there different treatments for different types of visitors?

5.   What foods are special or unique to your family?

6.   What name do you call your grandparents or other older relatives?

7.   What value have you learned from your parents?

8.   From what countries have your ancestors immigrated?

9. Identify a value held by grandparents that differs from you.

10. Identify a word or phrase that is unique or has a special meaning to your family.

11. What is the most common occupation held by members of your family?

12. List a topic or topics that would typically be discussed at family gatherings.

Questions:

1. How do your answers to the above questions reflect on your enculturation?

2. Assuming you have children now or in the future, which of the answers that you gave are your children likely to also give? Which ones are likely to be different? Why?

3. What questions in the assessment did you have difficulty in answering? Why was that the case? (For instance, if you don't know, where your ancestors immigrated from; what does that say about you, your family values, and cultural awareness?)

4. Try to compare your answers with other classmates or friends. In what way do your answers reflect similarity in your cultural backgrounds? In what way do they differ?

EXERCISE 4.3   AN INTERCULTURAL ENCOUNTER

Purpose:
1. To identify differences between you and someone from another culture.
2. To experience and analyze an intercultural interaction.

Directions:
1. Initiate an interaction with someone from a different culture. This might feel awkward and uncomfortable for you, but it will be well worth the effort. People are generally very open to talking to other people.
2. Try to carry on a conversation for at least five minutes. This can be done casually while you are walking across campus, sitting next to someone on the bus, or before class begins.
3. Ask questions that focus on interpersonal communication. You can ask about this person's experiences in assimilating to the United States. You might also ask what this person has found to be different in relationships and interactions from their native country. Be sure to gather the information you need to answer the questions below.
4. Pay attention both to the answers given to your questions and the way the two of you interact as well.

Questions:
1. What is this person's native country? How long has he or she been in the United States? Why is she or he here?

2. What major differences did you discover between you and this other person?

3. What similarities did you discover between you and this other person?

4. What difficulties would you anticipate if you tried to develop a relationship with this person?

5. How well do you think you would be able to assimilate into the other person's culture if you were to visit?

EXERCISE 4.4   DEVELOPING CULTURAL ELEMENTS

Purpose:
1. To become aware of how you learned the cultural elements that influence you.
2. To become aware of how you learned new cultural elements.

Directions:
1. Give an example for each of the following cultural elements that you have had for most of your life. Tell how you learned to value each.
2. List a newly acquired or learned example for each of the cultural elements.
3. Tell how you learned to value each.

ENCULTURATION EXAMPLES:

Material culture--a thing or an idea:

_____

_____

Social institutions--a school, government office, religious organization:

_____

_____

Individuals and the universe--a belief:

_____

_____

Aesthetics--a type of music, theater, art, dance:

_____

_____

Language--verbal and nonverbal communication pattern:

_____

_____

ACCULTURATION EXAMPLES:

Material culture--a thing or an idea:

_____

_____

Social institutions--a school, government office, religious organization:

_____

_____

Individuals and the universe--a belief:

_____

_____

Aesthetics--a type of music, theater, art, dance:

_____

_____

Language--verbal and nonverbal communication pattern:

_____

_____

EXERCISE 4.5   PLACING VALUE ON CULTURAL DIMENSIONS

Purpose:
1.   To understand how you learned your cultural values.
2.   To determine changes in your values.

Directions:
1.   For each of the following dimensions of cultural values, identify those values with which you were raised.
2.   How did the values you were raised with affect your communication and relationships with people from cultures?

DIMENSION

Masculine vs. Feminine

Values you were raised with: _____

_____

Effect on relationships: _____._____

_____

Individual vs. Group

Values you were raised with: _____

_____

Effect on relationships: _____

_____

Tolerance for Uncertainty vs. Need for Certainty

Values you were raised with: _____

_____

Effect on relationships: _____

_____

Concentrated vs. Decentralized Power

Values you were raised with: _____

_____

_____

Effects on relationships: _____

_____

_____

EXERCISE 4.6   DISCOVERING BARRIERS TO CULTURAL COMMUNICATION

Purpose:
1. To become aware of the barriers that inhibits effective intercultural communication.

Directions:
1. For each barrier listed below, describe two examples you have encountered or observed in your experiences.
2. Discuss how the example you give interfered with effective communication.

BARRIER

Ethnocentrism

1. Example encountered: _____

    _____

    Impact on communication: _____

    _____

2. Example encountered: _____

    _____

    Impact on communication: _____

    _____

Different Communication Codes

1. Example encountered: _____

    _____

    Impact on communication: _____

    _____

2. Example encountered: _____

    _____

    Impact on communication: _____

    _____

Stereotyping and Prejudice

1. Example encountered: _____

    _____

    Impact on communication: _____

    _____

2. Example encountered: _____

    _____

    Impact on communication: _____

    _____

Assuming Similarity

1. Example encountered: _____

    _____

    Impact on communication: _____

    _____

2. Example encountered: _____

    _____

    Impact on communication: _____

    _____

EXERCISE 4.7   MINDING YOUR MANNERS

Purpose:
1. To help you understand rules and manners for people in the United States.
2. To learn that expectations for manners differ from person to person even within the same culture.

Directions:
1. Identify the rules or expectations for behavior in response to each question.
2. Ask two other people (friends, classmates, or co-workers) for their responses and record their responses. Try to use someone from a different culture or who is at least from a background significantly different from yours.

Record your responses to the following questions:

How late can you be to a meeting without a reason and not be offensive? _____
_____

How do you expect to be greeted when meeting up with good friends? _____
_____

How would you greet a business or professional colleague: _____
_____

When is it appropriate to give gifts to friends and what types of gifts are appropriate?
_____
_____

When is it appropriate to give gifts to co-workers, employees, or supervisors and what types of gifts are appropriate? _____
_____

What are the typical times for breakfast, lunch, and dinner:_____
_____

When is it appropriate to use someone's first name?_____
_____

When is it inappropriate to use of someone's first name ? _____
_____

Record the responses of person 1 to the questions:
How late can you be to a meeting without a reason and not be offensive? _____
_____

How do you expect to be greeted when meeting up with good friends ?_____
_____

Person 1's Responses Continued

How would you greet a business or professional colleague: _____

_____

When is it appropriate to give gifts to friends and what types of gifts are appropriate?

_____

_____

When is it appropriate to give gifts to co-workers, employees, or supervisors and what
types of gifts are appropriate?

_____

_____

What are the typical times for breakfast, lunch, and dinner:_____

_____

When is it appropriate to use someone's first name?_____

_____

When is it inappropriate to use of someone's first name ? _____

_____

Record the responses of person 2 to the questions:

How late can you be to a meeting without a reason and not be offensive? _____

_____

How do you expect to be greeted when meeting up with good friends ?_____

_____

How would you greet a business or professional colleague: _____

_____

When is it appropriate to give gifts to friends and what types of gifts are appropriate?

_____

_____

When is it appropriate to give gifts to co-workers, employees, or supervisors and what
types of gifts are appropriate? _____

_____

What are the typical times for breakfast, lunch, and dinner:_____

_____

When is it appropriate to use someone's first name?_____

_____

When is it inappropriate to use of someone's first name ? _____

_____

Questions:

1. Which rules for manners are the most similar on the questionnaire responses?

2. Which rules are different?

3. What factors contribute to the differences among you and the other two respondents?

4. How have you come to learn the rules that you follow?

5. What rules have changed since you first learned them? What caused them to change?

6. How are the rules for behavior and their variations in the U. S. likely to impact effective communication for international visitors to the U.S.?

EXERCISE 4.8   ASSESSING YOUR ABILITY TO ADAPT

Purpose:
1.   To identify your ability to adapt to a variety of cultures.

Directions:
1.   Using the scale of 1 to 5, rate how strongly you agree with the statements below. One is low agreement and five is high agreement.
2.   Total your answers.

_____   1. I am constantly trying to understand myself better. I feel I know my strengths and weaknesses.

_____   2. I respect the opinions of others, though I may not always agree with them.

_____   3. I interact well with people who are very different from my self in age, race, economic status, and education.

_____   4. If I were at a party with people from other countries, I would normally go out of my way to meet them.

_____   5. I do not need to understand everything going on around me. I tolerate ambiguity.

_____   6. I am able to change course quickly. I readily change my plans or expectations to adapt to a new situation.

_____   7. I often find humor in difficult situations, and afterwards I can laugh at myself.

_____   8. When I have to wait, I am patient. I can be flexible with my agenda, schedule, or plans.

_____   9. I am always asking questions, reading, exploring. I am curious about new things, people, or places.

_____   10. I am resourceful and able to entertain myself.

_____   11. I tackle problems confidently without always needing the help of staff or spouse.

_____   12. When things go badly, I am able to keep my mind clear and my attitude positive.

_____ 13. I have made mistakes and learned from them.

_____ 14. In an unfamiliar situation, I watch and listen before acting.

_____ 15. I am a good listener.

_____ 16. When I am lost, I ask for directions.

_____ 17. I sincerely do not want to offend others.

_____ 18. I like people and accept them as they are.

_____ 19. I am sensitive to the feelings of others and observe their reactions when I am talking.

_____ 20. I like new ideas, new ways of doing things, and am willing to experiment.

Add the numbers you wrote next to each statement. If your score is 80 or above, you should be able to adapt well in a foreign culture. If your score is below 80, you will have to work to develop the attitude and behavior needed to make a good adjustment in a foreign culture. If your score is below 50, you should examine closely your decision regarding on overseas assignment or trip.

Questions:

1. What factors in your life have shaped your inclination to adapt to other people?

2. What could you do to increase your score?

EXERCISE 4.9   ADAPTING SLANG EXPRESSIONS

Purpose
1.   To increase your mindfulness about language use
2.   To practice interculturally adapting unclear and confusing expressions

Directions
1.   One common difficulty experienced by people from another country is understanding slang expressions. People are generally taught the literal meaning of words and therefore have difficulty with expressions that use the words in a slang expression. For each of the following "translate" the slang phrase into one that a person unfamiliar with it could understand.
2.   List of some of the idioms or slang phrases you commonly use and translate them.

Expressions	**Your Adapted "Translation"**
That's as easy as pie	_____
Finished in the nick of time	_____
Let's take a breather	_____
Let's grab a bite to eat	_____
He kicked the bucket	_____
She's a penny pincher	_____
We need to hit the books	_____

Your Typical Slang Expressions	**Your Adapted "Translation"**
1. _____	_____
2. _____	_____
3. _____	_____
4. _____	_____
5. _____	_____

EXERCISE 4.10   ASSESSING YOUR IMPRESSIONS OF OTHER CULTURES

Purpose:
1. To identify the impressions you have of other people and cultures
2. To identify stereotypes and prejudices that might affect your perception of others.

Directions:
1. For this exercise you need to write quickly, recording the first impression that comes to mind. Try to let your mind go free and avoid trying to think of the "best," "most correct," or "most appropriate" response. Be honest in your replies.
2. For each word write at least three constructs or qualities that you associate with it.

Culture	Three Qualities That Come To Your Mind:
Japanese	
Brazilian	
British	
Ghanaian	
German	
Afghani	
Korean	
French	
Somalian	
Israeli	

Questions:
1. Circle the words that have a negative connotation. To what degree is there a pattern to your use of negative terms?

2. What commonalities are there among the cultures that you have a positive impression of?

3. Examine your list and identify those that are based on grounded knowledge and observation and those that are not. What is the implication for stereotyping?

4. Which impressions would present the greatest challenge to effective interaction?

Globalization	Gender
Race	Ethnicity
Culture	Discrimination
Cultural Element	Sub-culture
Cultural Values	Enculturation
Feminine Culture	Masculine Culture

Socially learned and reinforced characteristics that include one's biological sex and psychological characteristics (femininity, masculinity, and androgyny).	The integration of economics and technology that is contributing to a worldwide, interconnected business environment.
Social classification based on nationality, religion, language, and ancestral heritage, shared by a group of people who also share a common geographical origin.	Genetically transmitted physical characteristics of a group of people.
Unfair or inappropriate treatment of people based on their group membership.	Learned system of knowledge, behavior, attitudes, beliefs, values, and norms that is shared by a group of people.
A microculture; a distinct cultural group that exists within a larger cultural context (such as, the gay and lesbian sub-culture).	Categories of things and ideas that identify the most profound aspects of cultural influence (such as schools, governments, music, theater, language).
Process of communicating a group's culture from generation to generation.	What a given group of people values or appreciates.
Culture that emphasizes achievement, assertiveness, heroism, and material wealth.	Culture that emphasizes relationships, caring for the less fortunate and overall quality of life.

Cultural Context	Acculturation
Low Context Culture	High Context Culture
Stereotype	Ethnocentrism
Intercultural Communication	Prejudice
Intercultural Communication Competence	Culture Shock
World View	Knowledge

Process through which an individual acquires new approaches, beliefs, and values by coming into contact with other cultures.	Information not explicitly communicated through language, but through environmental or nonverbal cues.
Culture that derives much information from nonverbal and environmental cues.	Culture that derives much information from the words of a message and less information from nonverbal and environmental cues.
Belief that your cultural traditions and assumptions are superior to those of others.	To place a person or group of persons into an inflexible, all-encompassing category.
A judgment or opinion of someone formed before you know all of the facts or background of that person.	Communication between or among people who have different cultural traditions.
Feelings of stress and anxiety a person experiences when encountering a culture different from his or her own.	Ability to adapt one's behavior toward another in ways that are appropriate to the other person's culture.
Information that enhances understanding of others; one of the elements necessary to becoming a competent communicator.	Individual perceptions or perceptions shared by a culture or group of people about key beliefs and issues, such as death, God, and the meaning of life, which influence interaction with others

Skill	Motivation
Third Culture	Social Decentering
Relational Empathy	Mindful
Empathy	Sympathy
Adapt	Communication Accommodation Theory
Adapt Predictively	Adapt Reactively

Internal state of readiness to respond to something.	Behavior that improves the effectiveness or quality of communicating with others.
Cognitive process in which we take into account another person's thoughts, feelings, values, background, and perspectives.	Common ground established when people from separate cultures create a third, "new," more comprehensive and inclusive culture.
Aware of cultural differences and the connection between thoughts and deeds in one's interactions with someone from a background different from one's own.	Essence of a relationship that permits varying degrees of understanding, rather than requiring complete comprehension of another's culture or emotions.
Acknowledgment that someone may be feeling bad; compassion toward someone.	Emotional reaction that is similar to the reaction being experienced by another person; empathizing is feeling what another person is feeling.
Theory that all people adapt their behavior to others to some extent.	To adjust one's behavior in accord with what someone else does. We can adapt based on the individual, the relationship, and the situation.
To modify or change behavior after an event.	To modify or change behavior in anticipation of an event.

CHAPTER 5
LISTENING AND RESPONDING SKILLS

OBJECTIVES

After studying the material in this chapter of *Interpersonal Communication: Relating to Others* and completing the exercises in this section of the study guide, you should understand:

1. The difference between hearing and listening.
2. How selecting, attending, understanding, remembering, and responding are part of the listening process.
3. The four listening styles.
4. How being self-absorbed, emotional noise, criticizing the speaker, rate of information, shifting attention, information overload, external noise, and listener apprehension all interfere with effective listening behavior.
5. The four levels of learning a skill and how they relate to listening.
6. How to improve your listening skills by stopping, looking, listening, asking questions, and reflecting content by paraphrasing.
7. How to respond with empathy by understanding your partner's feelings and by paraphrasing emotions.
8. The types of confirming responses and disconfirming responses.
9. How to improve critical listening and responding skills by identifying useful and flawed information, and avoiding jumping to conclusions.
10. And how to improve your responding skills by providing well-timed responses, providing useful information, avoiding unnecessary detail, and by being descriptive.

STUDY QUESTIONS

You should be able to answer the following questions:

1. What is the difference between hearing and listening?
2. What are the five elements of the listening process?
3. What are the four listening styles?
4. What are the barriers to effective listening?
5. Why do emotional "hot buttons" interfere with listening effectively?
6. How do the levels of learning a skill relate to listening behavior?
7. What are five ways you can improve your listening skills?
8. What does it mean to paraphrase?
9. What is the relationship between empathy and emotional intelligence?
10. What is a confirming response and a disconfirming response?
11. Explain how fact-inference confusion impairs critical listening.
12. How can you improve your responding skills?

EXERCISE 5.1   LISTENING COMPONENTS

Purposes:

1. To increase awareness of the components of listening: selecting, attending, understanding, remembering, and responding.

Directions:

1. Go to a website with videostreamed news features such as CNN.com or CBSnews.com.
2. Find a 1 or 2 minute news clip to play that primarily involves a summary report (not just a video of someone doing something). Play the clip but close your eyes and only listen to the broadcast. Ignore any introductory commercials and focus listening to the report.
3. After you have watched the clip, write down as completely as possible all that you heard:

4. Replay the video clip while looking at your notes above. Put a line through any pieces of information you wrote down that were inaccurate. Put a circle around any pieces of information for which you left out a lot of information. Write out any additional pieces of information from the clip that you missed altogether.

Questions:

1. What percentage of the original message were you able to capture in your first set of notes? What factors either inhibited or enhanced your completeness?

2. In what ways did the process of selecting affect what you heard?

3. In what ways did the process of attending affect what you heard?

4. In what ways did the process of remembering affect what you heard?

5. To what degree to your own self-interests affect your selection, attending, and remembering of the information you heard?

6. What aspects of the video clipped report caused you either miss information or to attend to particular information?

EXERCISE 5.2   LISTENING STYLES

Purposes:
1. To assess your listening style.
2. To examine how your listening style interacts with other people's listening styles.

Directions:
1. Read each of the four descriptions below and rank order them from the one that best describes you (as #1) to the one that least describes you (as #4.) Put your rankings in the column marked "ME."
2. Rank order each description on how well it describes a close friend of the same sex; put these rankings in the column marked "SSF" (Same Sex Friend).
3. Rank order each description on how well it describes a close friend of the opposite sex; put these rankings in the column marked "OSF" (Opposite Sex Friend.)
4. Rank order each description on how well it describes the parent or other relative with whom you sometimes have conflicts or misunderstanding. Put these rankings in the column marked "REL."

RANK ORDER

People Oriented Listener	ME	SSF	OSF	REL
1. Comfortable with and skilled at listening to people's feelings, and emotions.	___	___	___	___
2. Empathetic.	___	___	___	___
3. Looks for common interests.	___	___	___	___
4. Other-oriented; seeks strong interpersonal connections when listening.	___	___	___	___
5. Comfortable interacting inter-personally and in small groups.	___	___	___	___

Action Oriented Listener	ME	SSF	OSF	REL
1. Preference for well organized, brief, and error free information.	___	___	___	___
2. Dislikes long stories and hearing people digress.	___	___	___	___
3. Likes people to "get to the point."	___	___	___	___
4. Tends to be skeptical about what people have to say.	___	___	___	___
5. Second-guesses about the other person's ideas and assumptions rather than accepting things at face value.	___	___	___	___

Content Oriented Listener   **ME SSF OSF REL**

1. Comfortable listening to complex, detailed information.   ___ ___ ___ ___
2. Hones in on the facts, details, and evidence.   ___ ___ ___ ___
3. Rejects messages that lack sufficient supporting evidence
    and detail.   ___ ___ ___ ___
4. Good judge of accuracy and credibility of information.   ___ ___ ___ ___
5. Does some second-guessing.   ___ ___ ___ ___
6. Comfortable in groups and interpersonal interactions.   ___ ___ ___ ___

Time-Oriented Listener   **ME SSF OSF REL**

1. Keenly aware of how much time they have to listen.   ___ ___ ___ ___
2. Wants messages delivered quickly and briefly because
    they have a lot of things on their to-do list.   ___ ___ ___ ___
3. Not that interested in "visiting;" wants to get the message
    and move on.   ___ ___ ___ ___
4. Doesn't like rambling, or digressions.   ___ ___ ___ ___

Questions:

1. In what ways do your two strongest two listening styles affect how you interact with other people? How does it help? How does it hinder?

2. In what ways do your two strongest listening styles affect what you look for in your relationships with other people?

3. With whom do you have the most similar listening style? How does that similarity affect your interpersonal interactions with that person(s)? How does it affect your relationship(s)?

4. With whom do you have the most different listening style? How does that difference affect your interpersonal interactions with that person(s)? How does it affect your relationship(s)?

EXERCISE 5.3   LISTENING AND RELATIONSHIPS

Purposes:
1. To define listening
2. To compare listening ability and level of attraction to the listener.
3. To identify characteristics of effective and ineffective listeners.

Directions:
1. List the name of the two best listeners you know and their personal characteristics.
2. List the name of the two worst listeners you know and their personal characteristics.

Best Listeners	Characteristics
1._____	
2. _____	

Worst Listeners	Characteristics
1. _____	
2. _____	

Questions:
1. A. Do what degree are you attracted to each of the four individuals you listed?

    B. To what degree does their listening behavior affect your attraction toward them?

2. What impact does each person's listening abilities have on your relationship

3. Which characteristics are similar between the best listeners? The worst listeners?

4. Which characteristics are different between the best listeners? The worst listeners?

EXERCISE 5.4   TRIGGERING YOUR EMOTIONS

Purposes:
1. To identify the words, phrases, topics, and behaviors that create emotional reactions in you (positive or negatively).
2. To examine your listening effectiveness when hearing trigger words.

Directions:
1. List the words, phrases, topics, and behaviors that arouse your emotions.
2. Analyze how these words, phrases, and concepts interfere or enhance your listening effectiveness.

WORDS   **REACTIONS**

PHRASES   **REACTIONS**

TOPICS   **REACTIONS**

BEHAVIORS   **REACTIONS**

Questions:
1. What category are most of your "hot buttons" in--words, phrases, or topics?

2. What makes you have emotional reactions to the items you listed above--values, upbringing, etc.?

3. How can you control your reactions so that they do not interfere to your ability to listen to others effectively?

EXERCISE 5.5   INTERFERING BARRIERS TO YOUR LISTENING ABILITY

Purpose:

1. To become aware of the barriers preventing you from being an effective listener.

Directions:

1. For each of the following listening barriers, list the circumstances during which you have difficulty listening to others effectively.

Being self-absorbed: _____

_____

Unchecked emotions: _____

_____

Criticizing the speaker: _____

_____

Differing speech and thought rate: _____

_____

Shifting Attention: _____

_____

Information overload: _____

_____

External noise: _____

_____

Listener Apprehension: _____

_____

EXERCISE 5.6   ASSESSING YOUR COMPREHENSIVE LISTENING SKILLS

Purpose:
1. To understand what constitutes comprehensive listening skills.
2. To assess and improve your comprehensive listening skills.

Directions:
1. Select three of the comprehensive listening skills listed below on which you are weakest.
   - Stopping from focusing on you own messages and being other-centered.
   - Looking at the speaker's nonverbal cues.
   - Listening (not interrupting, responding appropriately while providing feedback, and contributing appropriately to the conversation),
   - Determining your listening goal
   - Transforming listening barriers into listening goals
   - Mentally summarizing details of the message
   - Weaving summaries into major/key points
   - Asking questions
2. Decide what you could do to improve each skill. Write the three skills on a card that you can carry with you and periodically review it before step 3.
3. Choose a specific comprehensive listening situation that you encounter and focus on engaging in the three skills you identified.

Questions:
1. To what degree did you improve in your use of these three listening skills?

2. What factors reduced your ability to improve?

3. Develop a plan for how you can improve these three skills in future interactions?

EXERCISE 5.7   PARAPHRASE RECOGNITION/PRACTICE

Purpose:
1. To help you recognize paraphrasing and practice it with others.

Directions:
1. Listen carefully during your interactions with others for examples of where the other people have paraphrased something another person has just said.
2. Record your observations as soon as possible.
3. During some of your interactions with other people, practice paraphrasing what they have said. Try to remember what you said and record your paraphrasing.

Observed Paraphrases

1. _____

_____

2. _____

_____

3. _____

_____

Examples of Your Paraphrases of Others.

1. _____

_____

2. _____

_____

3. _____

_____

EXERCISE 5.8   ASSESSING YOUR PARAPHRASING BEHAVIORS

Purpose:
1. To assess your paraphrasing skills and behaviors.
2. To help you decide which areas of behavior should be improved to increase your paraphrasing abilities.

Directions:
1. Respond to each statement below with a number as follows:

1 = **Always false**
2 = **Usually false**
3 = **Sometimes false; sometimes true**
4 = **Usually true**
5 = **Always true**

_____   1.   I maintain direct eye contact while listening to others.

_____   2.   When I listen, my body posture is open and relaxed

_____   3.   My arms and legs remain uncrossed when I am listening.

_____   4.   I use gestures and nod my head appropriately in response to other's comments.

_____   5.   I effectively use my face to express reactions to what I hear.

_____   6.   My voice tone and volume are adapted to the way the other person talks.

_____   7.   I am effective at asking appropriate follow-up questions.

_____   8.   I am particularly effective at accurately paraphrasing the content of what I hear.

_____   9.   I am particularly effective at accurately paraphrasing the emotions being expressed or felt by the other person.

_____   10. My paraphrasing is appropriately timed and does not interrupt the other.

_____   **TOTAL** of the scores in the 10 items.

A score of 40 to 50 indicates effective listening and paraphrasing. A score around 30 indicates some effectiveness, but a need for improvement. A score of less than 25 probably indicates a need for a more concentrated effort to improve.

Question:
1. Examine the individual items for those you have scored 3 or less on. What could you do to improve each of those behaviors?

EXERCISE 5.9   CREATING CONFIRMING RESPONSES

Purpose:
1. To help you practice creating responses that are confirming.
2. To help you identify when a response is disconfirming.

Directions:
1. For each of the following statements, write confirming responses that reflect the type of confirming responses listed by each statement.
2. Write a response where indicated that would be disconfirming.

A. "I'm really bummed. I was hoping to get my car back from the shop and they say it's going to be two more days and about $200 more than they originally told me."

1.) Confirming--Direct Acknowledgment:

2.) Confirming--Supportive Response:

3.) Disconfirming—Irrelevant Response:

B. "Wow, I can't believe how great I did on this paper. I really thought I had blown it, but the teacher really seemed to like it. Maybe, I'll make it through this course after all."

1.) Confirming—Expression of Positive Feeling:

2.) Confirming—Compliment:

3.) Disconfirming—Impersonal Response:

C. "When I was a kid my parents never got along very well. I used to get really scared when they would yell at each other. I hated it. I felt it was my fault they fought."

1.) Confirming—Clarifying Response:

2.) Confirming—Agreement about Judgment:

3.) Disconfirming—Tangential Response:

D. "I can't believe you like him! He's such an idiot. He always treats me like dirt. He's a real back stabber; he told me how much he appreciated me, and then he went around telling everyone else how worthless he thought I was."

1.) Confirming—Direct Acknowledgment:

2.) Confirming—Supportive Response:

3.) Disconfirming—Incongruous Response:

E. "I'm not sure about what we should do tonight. There are a couple of new movies that are opening tonight, but I'm not sure how exciting those are. Ruth Ann is having a party and she's invited us to come over if we want. What do you want to do?"

1.) Confirming—Clarifying Response:

2.) Confirming—Expression of Positive Feeling:

3.) Disconfirming—Incoherent Response:

EXERCISE 5.10   IMPROVING CRITICAL LISTENING AND RESPONDING SKILLS

Purpose:
1. To recognize the skills needed for critical listening and responding.
2. To assess difficulties you've experienced due to a breakdown in these skills.

Directions:
1. When the critical listening and responding skills listed in the text are not practiced, they can result in problems. List an instance where you have engaged in each failure listed in the appropriate column. If you can't think of an example of your own, use one you observed in others. Next indicate the impact on the speaker/relationship and what could be done to avoid the failure in the future.

Failure	Personal Instance	Impact	Plan for Avoiding
Failed to identify useful or flawed information			
Jumped to conclusions that were inaccurate.			
Mis-timed a response			
Provided unusable information			
Provided unnecessary details			
Gave an evaluative rather than descriptive response			

Listening	Asynchronous Listening
Selecting	Hearing
Understanding	Attending
Responding	Remembering
People-Oriented Listener	Listening Style
Second-Guessing	Action-Oriented Listener

Listening to someone's recorded message (on an answering machine or a cell phone) without the other person being present.	Process of selecting, attending to, creating meaning from, remembering, and responding to verbal and nonverbal messages.
Physiological process of decoding sounds.	Process of choosing one sound while sorting through various sounds competing for your attention.
Process of focusing on a particular sound or message.	Process of assigning meaning to sounds.
Process of recalling information.	Process of confirming your understanding of a message.
Preferred way of making sense out of spoken messages.	Listener who is comfortable with and skilled at listening to people's feelings and emotions.
Listener who prefers information that is well organized, brief, and error-free.	Questioning the ideas and assumptions underlying a message; assessing whether the message is true or false.

Time-Oriented Listener	Content-Oriented Listener
Emotional Noise	Ambush Listener
Meta-Message	Conversational Narcissism
Empathy	Paraphrase
Sympathy	Active Listening
Disconfirming Response	Confirming Response

Listener who is more comfortable listening to complex, detailed information than are those with other listening styles.	Listener who likes messages delivered succinctly.
Person who is overly critical and judgmental when listening to others.	Form of communication interference caused by emotional arousal
Focus on personal agendas and self-absorption rather than a focus on the needs and ideas of others.	A message about a message; the message a person is expressing via nonverbal means (such as by facial expressions, eye contact, and posture) about the message articulated in words.
Verbal summary of the key ideas of your partner's message that helps you check the accuracy of your understanding.	Feeling what others are feeling, rather than just acknowledging that they are feeling a certain way.
Interactive process of responding mentally, verbally, and nonverbally to a speaker's message.	Acknowledgment that someone is feeling bad; offer of support.
Statement that causes another person to value himself or herself more.	Statement that causes another person to value himself or herself less.

Social Support	Critical Listening
Information Triage	Fact
Inference	

Listening to evaluate and assess the quality, appropriateness, value, or importance of information.	Positive, sincere, supportive messages, both verbal and nonverbal, offered to help others deal with stress, anxiety, and uncertainty.
Something that has been directly observed to be true and thus has been proven to be true.	Process of evaluating information to sort good information from less useful or valid information
	Conclusion based on speculation

CHAPTER 6
VERBAL COMMUNICATION SKILLS

OBJECTIVES

After studying the material in this chapter of *Interpersonal Communication: Relating to Others* and completing the exercises in this section of the study guide, you should understand:

1. The relationship between words and their meanings.
2. How words influence us and our culture.
3. How to identify word barriers and know how to manage the barriers.
4. How the words we use affect our relationships with others.
5. The supportive approaches we can use when relating to others.
6. Being appropriately assertive.

STUDY QUESTIONS

You should be able to answer the following questions:

1. What are symbols, referents, and thoughts?
2. What does it mean when we say "words are arbitrary?"
3. How does culture impact the meaning of a symbol?
4. Explain how the theory of symbolic interactions relates to interpersonal communication.
5. Define denotative and connotative as they relate to words.
6. What does it mean when we say that words are abstract or concrete?
7. How do words have power to create, affect thoughts and actions, and affect and reflect culture?
8. Why are the following concepts considered barriers to understanding: bypassing, lack of precision, allness or indexing, static evaluation, polarization, and biased language?
9. What are the six ways you can use words help to establish supportive relationships?
10. Describe the five steps toward behaving assertively.

EXERCISE 6.1   WORDS, THOUGHTS, MEANINGS, AND BIASES

Purpose:
1. To examine the way you attribute meaning to the words you hear.
2. To recognize how the meanings you have reflect and affect your thinking.
3. To identify biased language.

Directions:
1. You are about to meet a new person and you are being told something about the person. Each word or phrase is what you've been told about the person.
2. Write down whatever thoughts come into your mind about this other person based upon the word or phrase.
3. Be as honest and open as you can about what comes to your mind.

What comes to your mind when you hear the person you are about to meet...

1. "is a jock." _____

2. "Is from New York City." _____

3. "is an 'Ag' major." _____

4. "Was adopted." _____

5. "Is named Bobbie Jo Jackson." _____

6. "Is a California blonde." _____

7. "Has HIV." _____

8. "Is a nerd." _____

9. "Is a secretary." _____

10. "Has a Ph. D." _____

<u>Questions:</u>

1. Which of meanings you assigned came from your personal experiences with people who fit the description? Which came from what friends and family have told you? Which came from the media (TV, movies, books)?

2. Which evoked negative meanings? Which evoked positive meanings? Why?

3. How many of the ten do you think of as women? As men? As neither? Why?

4. What do the meanings you assigned say about how you view other people? What biases might be affecting your responses?

5. What would it take to change the meaning you attached to each phrase from being the first thing you think of?

6. How might the meanings you attached affect your subsequent interaction with the person you are meeting?

EXERCISE 6.2   WORD TRACKER

Purpose:
1. To help understand how words work.
2. To understand how context affects the meaning of words.

Directions:
1. Over the next few days jot down any words you hear in conversation, lecture, TV, or which you read for which you initially didn't know the meaning or which was used in a way that is unfamiliar to you (this can include slang or jargon).
2. List at least five words you have heard here and the any meaning you inferred:

    Words   **Assumed Meaning**
    1.

    2.

    3.

    4.

    5.

3. Read the five words to two friends and write down what they think the words mean:
    1.

    2.

    3.

    4.

    5.

4. Look the words up in a dictionary or in a Web search and write a brief definition:
    1.

    2.

    3.

    4.

    5.

Questions:
1. Who was the most accurate in defining the term correctly? Why?

2. To what degree did the context of the word usage help you determine the meaning?

3. To what degree do you feel the dictionary meaning was really the one meant by the person who originally used the term you heard? Why?

EXERCISE 6.3   THE POWER OF WORDS TO CREATE: DR. SEUSS

Purpose:
1. To understand the arbitrary, abstract, and creative power of words.

Directions:
1. For this activity imagine you are writing your own short Dr. Seuss story. Write a paragraph using your imagination to describe a whimsical place that doesn't exist with creatures and objects that don't exist but do strange things. You can even make up your own words.
2. If you get the chance share your story with a classmate and listen to his or her story.

Your Story:

Questions:
1. To what degree could you create such a place if you didn't have words/symbols?

2. How far from reality can words take us?

3. What limits your ability to create stories that go outside the bounds of reality?

4. In sharing your story or hearing another's, how clearly was the image of the place you described conveyed?

EXERCISE 6.4   SPEAKING AMBIGUOUSLY

Purpose:
1.   To understand the problems of ambiguous language in creating clear messages.

Directions:
1.   Read the statements printed below.
2.   Answer the question following each statement in Column A.
3.   Have three other people (in Columns B, C, & D) answer the questions.
4.   Compare your answers.

STATEMENT	RESPONSES			
	A	B	C	D
1. James is independently wealthy. What is his total personal worth?	___	___	___	___
2. Mary is quite old. How old is Mary?	___	___	___	___
3. Jim is a heavy smoker. How many cigarettes does he smoke each day?	___	___	___	___
4. Carol watches a lot of television. How many hours a day does she spend watching TV?	___	___	___	___
5. David has been playing the guitar for a long time. How long had he been playing?	___	___	___	___
6. George, the plumber, is well paid for his service. What is his hourly wage?	___	___	___	___
7. Today is a very hot day. What is the temperature?	___	___	___	___
8. Professor Jones let us out of class quite early today. How many minutes prior to the normal dismissal time did the class finish?	___	___	___	___

Questions:
1.   What contributed to the differences in interpreting the meaning for the statements?

2.   How could you restate each statement, using more concrete language?

EXERCISE 6.5   CLEARING UP MY LANGUAGE

Purpose:
1. To examine your unclear language patterns in everyday communication events.
2. To learn others' perceptions of your unclear language patterns.

Directions:
1. For the next few days, keep a record of **your use** of jargon, words that might offend others, mispronounced or misused words, and repetitive and distracting words.
2. Afterwards, ask either those in the interaction or friends for their reaction (understanding and emotional response) to the language you listed.

JARGON OR RESTRICTED CODE: Words that have particular meaning only to a person, group or culture. Specialized terms or abbreviations.

Jargon/Restricted Code I Used   Other People's Reactions

1.

2.

3.

4.

BIASED LANGUAGE: Language reflecting gender, racial, ethnic, age, ability, or class biases. Words reflecting stereotypical attitudes and lack of sensitivity toward others.

Biased Language I Used   Other People's Reactions

1.

2.

3.

4.

STATIC EVALUATION: Pronouncement that does not take the possibility of change into consideration; use of labels and rigid categories.

Static Evaluations I Used   Other People's Reactions

1.

2.

3.

4.

<u>ALLNESS WORDS OR PHRASES:</u> Words or phrases that reflecting unqualified and often untrue generalizations.

Allness Word or Phrase I Used   Other People's Reactions

1.

2.

3.

4.

<u>POLARIZATION:</u> Words reflecting the use of bipolar extremes to describe and evaluate what you observe (good-bad, old-new, beautiful-ugly).

Polarized Term That I Used   Other People's Reactions

1.

2.

3.

4.

Questions:

1. In which categories did you find the most examples? Why?

2. To what degree did the reactions of others match or differ from your intended meaning behind the words and phrases you used?

3. What can you do to avoid or overcome these word barriers in the future?

EXERCISE 6.6   LANGUAGE AFFECTS OUR THOUGHTS

Purpose:
1. To increase your awareness of linguistic determinism and the Sapir-Whorf Hypothesis.
2. To assess how your own thinking has been affected by language.

Directions:
1. Identify terms or phrases that are used in your family or friends for a particular purpose of affecting your behavior.

Examples:
- "Cancer Sticks." Used by family member to describe cigarettes resulting in a negative feeling about smoking.
- "Organ donors on two wheels." Used by parents to describe motorcyclists to discourage their children from wanting to ride motorcycles.

Term or Phrase	Used by	Effect
A.		
B.		
C.		
D.		
E.		

Questions
1. To what degree to the terms or phrases actually affect your thinking/

2. What has influenced any changes in your thinking since you heard the phrase?

EXERCISE 6.7   TALKING IN CODES

Purpose:
1.   To help you understand how your language is unique to your relationships.

Directions:
1.   For this exercise relationships can be regarded as their own subcultures.
2.   Think of a close partner (romantic partner, family member, best friend).
3.   Think of a group in which you are a member (club, team, regular hang-out buddies).
3.   List the words, phrases, or other special language codes you use within each relationship.

PARTNER	GROUP

Questions:
1.   How did you and your partner develop your unique language codes?

2.   How did you feel about the group's language code when you first joined the group?

3.   How did you learn the special codes of the group to which you belong?

4.   Why don't you use the same language codes in other relationships?

5.   How do other people from outside the relationship or group react to the code?

EXERCISE 6.8   DESCRIBING WHAT YOU MEAN

Purpose:
1.   To practice turning static evaluation statements into descriptive statements.

Directions:
1.   Read the statements below.
2.   Rewrite each statement to describe the possible behavior(s) or characteristics that led to the original comment which labeled the person, object, or event include a dating reference (For example: "He's a rude person." becomes "He was really rude when I first met him.")

1.   "That teacher is a bore!"   _____

_____

_____

2.   "That guy's a real loser."   _____

_____

_____

3.   "Mike's a geek."   _____

_____

_____

4.   "LaKita is phat!"   _____

_____

_____

5.   "That car is sweet!"   _____

_____

_____

Questions:
1.   What was the biggest challenge about converting the statements?

2.   To what degree are your rewrites likely to reduce static evaluation?

EXERCISE 6.9   EXAMINING REGIONALISMS

Purpose:
1. To help you become aware of words having different meanings.

Directions:
1. Read all of the words referring to a given item.
2. Circle the word that you ordinarily use.
3. If you use more than one word in a group, mark the word you use most frequently.
4. Ask other people to share the word they use for each item described and put a mark by their choices. Choose people from different geographical locations and ages.

     A.   <u>What word do you use to describe the yard adjoining a barn:</u>

         1) Barn lot   2) Barnyard   3) Cow lot   4) Feed lot   5) Farm lot
         6) Other (specify) _____

     B.   <u>What word do you use to describe the heavy iron utensil for frying:</u>

         1) Frying pan   2) Skillet   3) Fry pan   4) Creeper   5) Spider
         6) Other (specify) _____

     C.   <u>What words do you use to describe the bone from a chicken breast:</u>

         1) Lucky bone   2) Pully bone   3) Wishbone   4) Breakbone   5) Pulling bone.
         6) Other (specify) _____

     D.   <u>What words do you use to describe the time when a clock shows 10:45</u>

         1) Quarter of eleven   2) Quarter to eleven   3) Quarter till eleven   5) Ten Forty-Five   6) Almost eleven   7) Other (specify) _____

     E.   <u>What word do you use to describe the paper container used for groceries:</u>

         1) A Bag   2) A Tote   3) Grocery sack   4) Grocery bag   5) Sack   6) Poke
         7) Other (specify) _____

     F.   <u>What word do you use to describe corn eaten on cob:</u>

         1) Corn-on-the-cob   2) Green corn   3) Sweet corn   4) Roasting ears
         5) Sugar corn   6) Garden corn   7) Other (specify) _____

     G.   <u>What word do you use to describe the worm used for bait in fishing:</u>

         1) Angleworm   2) Fish worm   3) Fishing worm   4) Red worm   5) Earthworm.
         6) Fish bait   7) Night crawlers   8) Other (specify) _____

     H.   <u>What word do you use to describe the family word for father:</u>

         1) Dad   2) Daddy   3) Father   4) Pa   5) Papa   6) Pappy   7) Paw   8) Pop
         9) Other (specify) _____

I. <u>What word do you use to describe the family word for mother:</u>

1) Ma 2) Mama 3) Maw 4) Mom 5) Mum 6) Mommy
7) Mother 8) Mammy 9) Other (specify) _____

J. <u>What phrase do you use to describe the summer work on a grass in a yard:</u>

1) Cut the grass 2) Cut the yard 3) Cut the lawn 4) Mow the grass
5) Mow the yard 6) Mow the lawn 7) Other (specify) _____

K. <u>What do you typically say when greeting people:</u>

1) Hello 2) Hi 3) Howdy 4) What's up? 5) Whasup? 6) Hey 7) Yo
8) Sup 9) What's happening? 10) How's it going? 11) How are you?
12) Hola 13) Other (specify) _____

Questions:

1. To what degree are your responses similar or different than the other people's?

2. Explain why responses were either similar or different.

3. What impact might these differences have when you are interacting with other people?

4. What other words or phrases do you use that are unique to your region?

EXERCISE 6.10   ASSERTIVENESS AND AGGRESSIVENESS

Purpose:
1.   To learn the difference between assertiveness and aggressiveness

Directions:
1.   Each scenario involves aggressiveness. Using the five steps from the chapter for being assertive, write an assertive response to replace the aggressive one.

The Restaurant Salad: You are eating at a very busy restaurant and have been waiting a long time for your order to arrive. Finally your salad arrives and you say, "What the heck is this garbage? I didn't order coleslaw—I wanted a spinach salad. You're the most incompetent waiter I've ever seen. Get this pig slop off the table and bring me my salad, NOW!!!"

Your alternative assertive reply:

The Late Pickup: A friend is an hour late to pick you up to go out to eat. You declare, "You're the most unreliable person I have ever known. Why I agreed to go out to eat with you is beyond me. Now we're going to hit the crowds and have to wait an hour just for a table. Don't just stand there, let's get going!!!"

Your alternative assertive reply:

The "D" Paper: You've gotten a "D" on a paper in a required class that you hate with an instructor you dislike. Here's what you say to the instructor: "I can't believe you dumped on me like this. I worked hard but you gave such lousy instructions no one knew what to do. I've never gotten below a "B" on a paper before from any *good* instructor."

Your alternative assertive reply:

Spring Break: Your parents want you to come home over spring break, and you want to go with some friends on a spring trip. You declare, "I'm going with my friends; I don't care what you want. You can't tell me what to do anymore. You two are so selfish and insensitive. None of my friends has parents as controlling and demanding as you two."

Your alternative assertive reply:

Symbol	Referent
Thought	Symbolic Interaction Theory
Linguistic Relativity	Sapir-Whorf Hypothesis
Denotative Meaning	Connotative Meaning
Linguistic Determinism	World View
Bypassing	Malapropism

Thing that a symbol represents.	Word, sound, or visual device that represents an image, sound, concept or experience.
Theory that members of a society are bound together through common use of symbols.	Mental process of creating an image, sound, concept, or experience triggered by a referent or symbol.
Based on the principles of linguistic determinism and linguistic relativity, the hypothesis that language shapes our thoughts and culture, and our culture and thoughts affect the language we use to describe our world.	Theory that each language includes some unique features that are not found in other languages.
Personal and subjective meaning of a word.	Restrictive or literal meaning of a word.
Culturally acquired perspective for interpreting experiences.	Theory that describes how use of language determines or influences thoughts and perceptions.
Confusion of one word or phrase for another that sounds similar to it.	Confusion caused by the same words meaning different things to different people

Restricted Code	Jargon
Allness	Indexing
Static Evaluation	Polarization
Elaborated Code	Word Picture
Assertive	Aggressive
Extended *I* Language	Apology

Another name for restricted code: specialized terms or abbreviations whose meanings are known only to members of a specific group.	Set of words that have particular meaning to a person, group, or culture.
Avoiding generalizations by using statements that separate one situation, person, or example from another.	Tendency to use language to make unqualified, often untrue generalizations.
Description and evaluation of what you observe in terms of extremes such as good or bad, old or new, beautiful or ugly.	Pronouncement that does not take the possibility of change into consideration.
Short statement or story that illustrates or describes an emotion; word pictures often use a simile (a comparison using the word *like* or *as*) to clarify the image.	Conversation that uses many words and various ways of describing an idea or concept to communicate its meaning.
Expressing one's interests while denying the rights of others by blaming, judging, and evaluating other people.	Able to pursue one's own best interests without denying a partner's rights.
Explicit admission of an error, along with a request for forgiveness.	Brief preface to a feedback statement, intended to communicate that you don't want your listener to take your message in an overly critical way.

CHAPTER 7
NONVERBAL COMMUNICATION SKILLS

OBJECTIVES

After studying the material in this chapter of *Interpersonal Communication: Relating to Others* and completing the exercises in this section of the study guide, you should understand:

1. The importance of studying nonverbal communication because it communicates our feelings and attitudes, it is more believable than verbal messages, it interacts with the meaning of verbal messages, we respond and adapt through it, and it plays a major role in our interpersonal relationships.
2. The challenge of interpreting nonverbal communication because it is ambiguous, continuous, multichanneled, and culture based nonverbal communication.
3. The different nonverbal communication codes (body movement, eye contact, facial expression, vocal cues, personal space, territory, touch, and appearance) that are used to communicate messages.
4. How to interpret immediacy, arousal, and dominance messages.
5. How to improve your ability to interpret messages by considering the context of the message, looking for clusters of clues, using past experiences with the other person, checking your perceptions of messages with others, being aware that emotions are contagious, and look for cues about lying.

STUDY QUESTIONS

You should be able to answer the following questions:

1. Why is it important to learn about nonverbal communication?
2. Why is nonverbal communication difficult and challenging to interpret?
3. Identify the nonverbal communication codes.
4. What are the different categories/functions of body movement and gestures?
5. What are the four functions for eye contact in interpersonal interactions?
6. What are the six primary emotional categories that identify our facial expressions?
7. How is the voice a primary tool for communicating information about relationships?
8. Describe Edward Hall's four spatial zones?
9. Why is the use of touch important and when are we likely to initiate the use of touch with others?
10. How does personal appearance relate to interpersonal interactions?
11. Describe Mehrabian's three dimensions used to interpret nonverbal cues?
12. What is expectancy violation theory?
13. How can you improve your ability to interpret nonverbal messages?
14. What are some differences between honest and dishonest communicators?

EXERCISE 7.1   FORMING FIRST IMPRESSIONS

Purpose:
1. To become aware of the nonverbal cues that you use in making first impressions.

Directions:
1. Go to a public place--shopping center, library, campus shopping area, etc.
2. Observe three different people.
3. Fill out the following survey form by providing what you believe is the quality and the nonverbal cues on which you based that judgment.
4. Optional: Check out your impressions by approaching the person, explaining what you are doing, and asking to provide information for each quality.

PERSON #1

Personal Quality	**Nonverbal Cues**
AGE:	
OCCUPATION:	
POLITICAL ORIENTATION:	
MUSIC PREFERENCE:	
FAVORITE PASTIME:	
RELIGIOUS AFFILIATION:	
RELATIONSHIP TO OTHERS:	

PERSONALITY CHARACTERISTICS (outgoing, athletic, shy, funny, intelligent, etc.):

PERSON #2

Personal Quality	**Nonverbal Cues**
AGE:	
OCCUPATION:	

PERSON #2 (continued)

POLITICAL ORIENTATION:

MUSIC PREFERENCE:

FAVORITE PASTIME:

RELIGIOUS AFFILIATION:

RELATIONSHIP TO OTHERS:

PERSONALITY CHARACTERISTICS (outgoing, athletic, shy, funny, intelligent, etc.):

PERSON #3

Personal Quality　　　　**Nonverbal Cues**

AGE:

OCCUPATION:

POLITICAL ORIENTATION:

MUSIC PREFERENCE:

FAVORITE PASTIME:

RELIGIOUS AFFILIATION:

RELATIONSHIP TO OTHERS:

PERSONALITY CHARACTERISTICS (outgoing, athletic, shy, funny, intelligent, etc.):

Questions:

1. On what nonverbal cues did you depend on the most? The least?

2. How confident are you about the accuracy of your judgments?

3. What was the most difficult quality to judge? Why?

4. What was the easiest quality to judge? Why?

EXERCISE 7.2   CONFUSING NONVERBAL COMMUNICATION

Purposes:
1. To understand the ambiguity of nonverbal communication.
2. To monitor your own nonverbal behavior.

Directions:
1. Monitor your communication interactions for the next few days.
2. Report on three interpersonal interactions where there were communication problems associated with your nonverbal behaviors.
3. Use the following form to report your observations.

INTERACTION #1:

TIME: _____

PLACE: _____

RELATIONSHIP TO THE OTHER PERSON: _____

YOUR NONVERBAL CUE THAT CREATED THE PROBLEM: _____

_____

TYPE OF PROBLEM: _____

_____

EFFECTS OR OUTCOME OF PROBLEM: _____

_____

HOW COULD THE PROBLEM HAVE BEEN AVOIDED? _____

_____

INTERACTION #2:

TIME: _____

PLACE: _____

RELATIONSHIP TO THE OTHER PERSON: _____

_____

YOUR NONVERBAL CUE THAT CREATED THE PROBLEM: _____

_____

TYPE OF PROBLEM: _____

_____

EFFECTS OR OUTCOME OF PROBLEM: _____

_____

HOW COULD THE PROBLEM HAVE BEEN AVOIDED? _____

_____

INTERACTION #3:

TIME: _____

PLACE: _____

RELATIONSHIP TO THE OTHER PERSON: _____

YOUR NONVERBAL CUE THAT CREATED THE PROBLEM: _____

_____

TYPE OF PROBLEM: _____

_____

EFFECTS OR OUTCOME OF PROBLEM: _____

_____

HOW COULD THE PROBLEM HAVE BEEN AVOIDED? _____

_____

EXERCISE 7.3   CHALLENGING CONCLUSIONS

Purpose:
1. To investigate the difficulty in making accurate interpretations of nonverbal behavior.
2. To determine the effect the relationship has on the accuracy of interpretations.

Directions:
1. For the next few days, observe the nonverbal behavior of five people (friends, family members, co-workers) focusing on specific occurrences/situations and specific nonverbal behavior for each observation.
2. Record your interpretation of each person's nonverbal behavior.
3. Share your interpretations with the other people to assess your accuracy in comparison with their explanation.

Relationship	Situation/ Behavior	Interpretation of Nonverbal	Other's Explanation
1.			
2.			
3.			
4.			
5.			

Questions:

1. How did your accuracy of interpretation relate to the level of closeness in your relationship with the other people?

2. How did your interpretations compare to the explanations of the others?

3. What behaviors were the most confusing for you? Why?

4. What behaviors were the easiest to interpret accurately? Why?

5. In what ways did the situation influence your interpretation of the nonverbal behaviors?

EXERCISE 7.4   NONVERBAL CHARADES

Purposes:
1.   To understand how nonverbal messages substitute for verbal messages.
2.   To practice your own nonverbal expressivity.

Directions:
1.   Ideally, this would be a good activity to do with a friend or classmate. Communicate each message using only nonverbal cues (you can use your voice, but you are limited to saying the word "Bananas." Have your partner guess what the message is you are communicating.
2.   If you are doing this on your own, use a mirror to see your expressions.
3.   Record the ways that you used to express the message.

Verbal Message	**Nonverbal Cues used to Express the Message**
A. "I'm afraid"	
B. "Don't bother me right now"	
C. "I'd really like to get to know you better."	
D. "I'm too tired to talk anymore."	
E. "I'm excited and I have something important to tell you."	
F. "What are you looking at me like that? I haven't done anything wrong."	

Questions:
1. Which messages were easiest to convey? Why?

2. What nonverbal codes did you rely on the most? Why?

3. How accurately was your partner able to understand your message (or probably would)?

EXERCISE 7.5   VIOLATING NONVERBAL EXPECTANCIES

Purpose:
1. To recognize the importance of expectancy violation theory.

Directions:
1. Identify three nonverbal expectations that exist in your interactions with others (friends, other students, family members, co-workers, etc).

    #### Three Expectancies
    1.

    2.

    3.

2. Choose one expectation from your list and violate that expectation. Ethically, you should not break an expectation that infringes on the rights of the other person!
3. Engage in the violating nonverbal behavior during interactions with three different people and describe how they behaved, if any, of the other person. Ask the other person if they noticed the violation and how they felt. Record the results here:

Other's Behaviors	Other's Thoughts/Feelings
Person #1:	
Person # 2	
Person #3	

Questions:
1. In what ways did the other people adapt to your violation?

2. What factors in your three relationships might have affected the other person's reactions?

3. In what ways would continuing the violation affect your relationships?

EXERCISE 7.6   SENSITIVTY TO TOUCH

Purpose:
1.   To recognize your varying levels of comfort with being touched.

Directions:
1.   In the space before each item, indicate the degree to which you are comfortable or uncomfortable with the touch described using the following scale:

1 = Comfortable   2 = Neutral   3 = Uncomfortable

_____ Someone's arm touching your's while standing in a crowded elevator

_____ A casual friend of the opposite sex putting a hand on your shoulder while asking a favor.

_____ A close friend of the same sex putting his or her arm on your shoulder while sharing very personal information.

_____ A student of the opposite sex that you sit by in class grabbing your arm and holding it when he or she excitedly tells you of his or her great grade on the paper just returned.

_____ A person you are seeing romantically reaching out to touch you while you are sitting together watching a TV program

_____ Your spouse reaching out to touch you while you are sitting together watching a TV program.

_____ Receiving a hug from a family member you don't know very well.

_____ Receiving a hug from your mother when you return home from a trip.

_____ Receiving a hug from your father when you return home from a trip.

_____ Being patted on the back/shoulder as you say goodbye to a same sex friend.

_____ Being patted on the butt by a teammate after you made a good play.

_____ The side of your thigh touching a stranger's thigh while sitting next to you on a crowded plane or bus.

_____ TOTAL THE SCORES. Score will be between 12 and 36.

Questions:
1.   Overall does your score indicate whether you are generally comfortable or uncomfortable with touch? How satisfied are you with your level of comfort? Why?

2.   What patterns do you notice among those items on which you scored high or low?

3.   What factors in your life have contributed to your responses to touch listed above?

EXERCISE 7.7   MONITORING YOUR NONVERBAL BEHAVIOR

Purpose:
1. To recognize how you use nonverbal behavior to express emotions.

Directions:
1. Over the next few days, pay attention to the different emotions you are feeling.
2. Monitor the nonverbal expressions of each emotion and record the results in the form below.
3. Pay attention to how other people react to you when you are feeling these emotions.
4. If you get the chance, ask the others what they think you are feeling and what nonverbal cues they were responding to.

Situation # 1: _____

a.) Emotion I was feeling:

b.) Nonverbal cues I exhibited:

c.) How other people reacted to me:

d.) What other people thought I was feeling:

e.) Nonverbal cues other people said they noticed:

Situation # 2: _____

a.) Emotion I was feeling:

b.) Nonverbal cues I exhibited:

c.) How other people reacted to me:

d.) What other people thought I was feeling:

e.) Nonverbal cues other people said they noticed:

Situation # 3: _____

a.) Emotion I was feeling:

b.) Nonverbal cues I exhibited:

c.) How other people reacted to me:

d.) What other people thought I was feeling:

e.) Nonverbal cues other people said they noticed:

Situation # 4: _____

a.) Emotion I was feeling:

b.) Nonverbal cues I exhibited:

c.) How other people reacted to me:

d.) What other people thought I was feeling:

e.) Nonverbal cues other people said they noticed:

Questions:

1. To what degree did you have a hard time recognizing your own emotional state?

2. How well were other people able to identify your feelings from your nonverbal cues?

3. Overall, how emotional expressive do you think you are? What makes you think this?

EXERCISE 7.8   INTERPRETING THE PRIMARY DIMENSIONS OF NONVERBAL CUES

Purpose:

1. To learn to recognize examples of immediacy (liking), arousal (responding), and dominance (power).

Directions:

1. Observe pairs of people interacting at work, at home, or at school. Use from two to six different couples depending on which dimensions are demonstrated.
2. Record nonverbal behaviors that indicate a **high** level of immediacy between two of the individuals in two different couples.
3. Record nonverbal behaviors that indicate a **high** level of arousal between the individuals in two different couples.
4. Record nonverbal behaviors that indicate a **high** level of dominance between the individuals in two different couples.

COUPLE #1	COUPLE #2

IMMEDIACY

COUPLE #1	COUPLE #2
Posture _____	Posture _____
Body orientation _____	Body orientation _____
Eye contact _____	Eye contact _____
Gestures _____	Gestures _____
Movement _____	Movement _____
Touch _____	Touch _____
Space _____	Space _____
Voice _____	Voice _____
Facial Expression _____	Facial Expression _____

AROUSAL

Posture _____   Posture _____

Body orientation _____   Body orientation _____

Eye contact _____   Eye contact _____

Gestures _____   Gestures _____

Movement _____   Movement _____

Touch   _____   Touch _____

Space _____   Space _____

Voice _____   Voice _____

Facial Expression _____   Facial Expression _____

DOMINANCE

Posture _____   Posture _____

Body orientation _____   Body orientation _____

Eye contact _____   Eye contact _____

Gestures _____   Gestures _____

Movement _____   Movement _____

Touch   _____   Touch _____

Space _____   Space _____

Voice _____   Voice _____

Facial Expression _____   Facial Expression _____

Questions

1. What were the most common ways that you observed for displaying immediacy?

2. What were the most common ways that you observed for displaying arousal?

3. What were the most common ways that you observed for displaying dominance?

4. Which of the three dimensions was most difficult to observe? Why?

5. Which nonverbal codes were least used? Why do you suppose that was?

6. To what degree do you see the nonverbal behaviors and the observations of the three dimensions relating to the relationship satisfaction of the partners?

EXERCISE 7.9   VOICE LESSONS

Purpose:
1. To determine how vocal characteristics affect perception.

Directions:
1. Turn on a television show that you have never watched before and tape the show.
2. Go to another room where you cannot see the television, but you can hear the voices.
3. Listen to the voices of two actors or speakers for five or ten minutes.
4. Write a description of each person, including information such as gender, age, race, educational background, occupation, status, and emotional state.
5. Rewind and play the tape of the show to determine how accurate your description is (you might do a Web search for other confirming information about the characters)

DESCRIPTION (age, sex, race, occupation, marital status, status, etc.)

ACTOR #1

ACTOR #2

Questions:
1. How accurate were you with your descriptions?

2. What vocal cues did you attend to in creating your descriptions?

3. What misjudgments about others occurred because of relying only vocal cues?

4. What judgments are people likely to make about you based only on your vocal cues?

5. What vocal qualities do you find particularly irritating? Pleasing?

EXERCISE 7.10   COMMUNICATING ABOUT YOU IN YOUR PLACE

Purposes:
1. To understand territorial markers.
2. To investigate what your "place" communicates about you.

Directions:
1. Identify a place that you consider to be yours--bedroom, kitchen, den, office, or residence hall room, and answer the questions that follow.

"YOUR" PLACE

1. How have you decorated the space (Pictures, posters, furniture, stereo, curios, etc)?

2. What inferences might a stranger make about you after observing these decorations?

3. What things do you have sitting around that are yours and that might give a stranger clues about you? (Magazines, books, dirty laundry, empty potato chip bags, etc.)

4. What inferences might a stranger make about you after observing these artifacts?

5. How does the arrangement of the furniture affect interpersonal interactions (promote or inhibit)? Why?

6. How could you rearrange the furniture to facilitate better interpersonal interactions?

7. What territorial markers do you use to let others know what is your space?

EXERCISE 7.11 ANALYZING SALES PEOPLE

Purpose:
1. To become aware of the positive and negative nonverbal behaviors used by sales people.
2. To become aware of your personal reaction to nonverbal behaviors of sales people.

Directions:
1. Observe 2 different sales persons during a shopping trip.
2. Fill out the following chart, regarding the nonverbal behaviors of each of the sales people.

Behaviors	Sales Person #1	Sales Person #2
Eye Behaviors:		
+ Sustained eye contact with the customer	Yes No	Yes No
+ Looked directly at the customer	Yes No	Yes No
- Looked down or away before making a point	Yes No	Yes No
- Exhibited shifty eyes	Yes No	Yes No
- Blinked excessively	Yes No	Yes No
Gestures:		
+ Used hand and head gestures to emphasize a point	Yes No	Yes No
+ Used gestures to signal a desire to continue talking	Yes No	Yes No
+ Kept hands and elbows out and away from the body	Yes No	Yes No
+ Avoided using distracting hand-to-face gestures	Yes No	Yes No
- Exhibited any weak and tentative gestures	Yes No	Yes No
- Cleared throat excessively	Yes No	Yes No
- Smiled out of context	Yes No	Yes No
- Fidgeted	Yes No	Yes No
- Put hands in pockets or on objects in the room	Yes No	Yes No
Posture:		
+ Assumed an open and relaxed posture	Yes No	Yes No
+ Used postural shifts to indicate interest	Yes No	Yes No
+ Leaned forward while making a point	Yes No	Yes No
+ Faced the customer directly	Yes No	Yes No
- Exhibited bodily tension	Yes No	Yes No
- Appeared rigid	Yes No	Yes No
- Communicated with crossed arms/legs	Yes No	Yes No

Behaviors	Sales Person #1	Sales Person #2
Vocal cues:		
+ Used a conversational speaking style	Yes No	Yes No
+ Emphasized important points with change in pitch	Yes No	Yes No
+ Communicated with sufficient volume	Yes No	Yes No
+ Spoke at an appropriate rate	Yes No	Yes No
- Spoke with a limited pitch variation	Yes No	Yes No
- Sounded flat, tense, or nasal	Yes No	Yes No
- Paused at length before answering questions	Yes No	Yes No
- Used non-fluencies and word repetitions	Yes No	Yes No
- Interrupted the customer	Yes No	Yes No

Questions:

1. Which positive behaviors were used most often?

2. Which negative behaviors were used most often?

3. To what degree would each sales person's nonverbal behaviors affect your willingness to make a purchase from each?

4. Which of the behaviors were most distracting to you? Why?

5. What nonverbal behaviors, if any, do you think the sales people were intentionally displaying?

EXERCISE 7.12   SPACE SCAVENGER HUNT

Purpose:
1.   To become aware of how space is used to communicate.
2.   To increase awareness of how we manage violations of expectations.

Directions:
1.   Fill in the following scavenger hunt sheet over the next couple of days using your observations of space and territory.

Where observed?	Use of space and observed behaviors
An intimate couple	
A couple that is angry at each other	
Two people involved in a business transaction (customer-server)	
Two strangers forced by circumstance to be physically nearer than they intended	
People choosing their seats in an uncrowded fast food joint.	

Questions:
1. How important does space seem to be in the above situations? For which was it most important? Least?

2. What violations to spatial expectations did you observe? How did people respond to them?

EXERCISE 7.13   NONVERBAL SENSITIVITY AND PERCEPTION CHECKING

Purpose:
1. To examine your sensitivity to other people's nonverbal messages.
2. To practice perception checking.

Directions:
1. As you is interacting with your friends over the next few days. Make a mental note of what you believe is their emotional state at any given moment.
2. Think about what nonverbal cues you are responding to.
3. Tell your friends your perceptions. Tell them what nonverbal cues you picked up and your interpretations (emotion). Ask them to tell you if you are accurate or not. Be open to continuing the discussion and practice your empathic listening.
4. Record the events below.

Situation #1:
a) What were the nonverbal cues you observed?

b) What emotion did you believe your friend was experiencing?

c) What emotion did your friend claim to be experiencing?

d) What lead to your observation being accurate or inaccurate?

Situation #2:
a) What were the nonverbal cues you observed?

b) What emotion did you believe your friend was experiencing?

c) What emotion did your friend claim to be experiencing?

d) What lead to your observation being accurate or inaccurate?

Situation #3:
a) What were the nonverbal cues you observed?

b) What emotion did you believe your friend was experiencing?

c) What emotion did your friend claim to be experiencing?

d) What lead to your observation being accurate or inaccurate?

Situation #4:
a) What were the nonverbal cues you observed?

b) What emotion did you believe your friend was experiencing?

c) What emotion did your friend claim to be experiencing?

d) What lead to your observation being accurate or inaccurate?

Questions:

1. Overall, how would you rate your ability to pick up on nonverbal cues reflecting others' emotional states?

2. What nonverbal cues did you tend to rely on the most?

3. What nonverbal cues did you tend to miss or misinterpret the most?

4. What could you do to improve your accuracy in assessing other people's emotional state?

Nonverbal Communication	Interaction Adaptation Theory
Emblems	Interactional Synchrony
Affect Display	Kinesics
Adaptors	Illustrators
Back Channel Cues	Regulators
Intimate Space	Proxemics

A theory suggesting that people interact with others by adapting their communication behavior.	Behavior other than written or spoken language that creates meaning for someone.
Mirroring of each other's nonverbal behavior by communication partners.	Nonverbal cues that have specific, generally understood meaning in a given culture and may substitute for a word or phrase
Study of human movement and gestures.	Nonverbal behavior that communicates emotions
Nonverbal behaviors that accompany a verbal message and either contradict, accent, or complement it.	Nonverbal behaviors that satisfy a personal need and help a person adapt or respond to the immediate situation.
Nonverbal messages that help to control the interaction or flow of communication between people.	Vocal cues that signal your wish to speak or not to speak.
Study of how close or far away from people and objects people position themselves.	Zone of space most often used for very personal or intimate interactions, ranging from 0 to 1 ½ feet from the individual.

Social Space	Personal Space
Territoriality	Public Space
Territorial Markers	Immediacy
Arousal	Dominance
Expectancy Violation Theory	Perception Checking
Emotional Contagion Theory	

Zone of space most often used for conversations with family and friends, ranging from 1 1/2 to 4 feet from the individual.	Zone of space most often used for group interactions, ranging from 4 to 12 feet from the individual.
Zone of space most often used by public speakers or anyone speaking to many people, ranging beyond 12 feet from the individual.	Study of how animals and humans use space and objects to communicate occupancy or ownership of space
Feelings of liking, pleasure, and closeness communicated by such nonverbal cues as eye contact, forward lean, touch, and open body orientation.	Tangible objects that are used to signify that someone has claimed an area or space.
Power, status, and control communicated by such nonverbal cues as a relaxed posture, greater personal space, and protected personal space.	Feelings of interest and excitement communicated by such nonverbal cues as vocal expressions, facial expressions, and gestures.
Asking someone whether your interpretation of his or her nonverbal behavior is accurate.	Theory that you interpret the messages of others based on how you expect others to behave.
	Theory that emotional expression is contagious; people can "catch" emotions just by observing other's emotional expressions.

CHAPTER 8
CONFLICT MANAGEMENT SKILLS

OBJECTIVES

After studying the material in this chapter of *Interpersonal Communication: Relating to Others* and completing the exercises in this section of the study guide, you should understand:

1. How the definition of conflict relates to interpersonal communication.
2. The source of the commonly held myths about interpersonal conflict.
3. How conflict operates as a process going through five stages.
4. The differences between the three types of interpersonal conflict.
4. The differences between destructive and constructive approaches to conflict management.
6. The basic elements of the five conflict management styles.
7. The conflict management skills of managing your emotions, information, goals, and problems.
8. Strategies for dealing with prickly people.

STUDY QUESTIONS

You should be able to answer the following questions:

1. What is conflict?
2. What are the commonly held myths about interpersonal conflict and where did they originate?
3. How are pseudo conflict, simple conflict, and ego conflict the same and different?
4. Describe the five stages of the conflict process and explain the communication behaviors that occur in each stage.
5. What are the five types of conflict management styles and what communication behaviors are exhibited with each style?
6. What skills can you use to manage your emotions in a conflict?
7. What skills are needed to manage information during a conflict?
8. What steps are needed in managing the goals and the problem?
9. How do you deal with prickly people?

EXERCISE 8.1   AN INTERPERSONAL CONFLICT LOG AND ANALYSIS

Purpose:
1. To recognize interpersonal problems and conflicts that occur in your life.
2. To understand the elements that make something an interpersonal conflict.
2. To assess the differences in intensity among your conflicts.

Directions:
1. For each of the next four days keep track of all the disagreements, struggles, arguments, challenges, fights, and interference in getting something that you want.
2. Write a very brief tag line to describe the situation; for example, "Joe cancelled on going to the game with me" or "Maria ignored me when I tried to talk to her." Don't write in the blanks that appear at the beginning of each line.

First Day:
_____ _____ _____ 1.
_____ _____ _____ 2.
_____ _____ _____ 3.
_____ _____ _____ 4.
_____ _____ _____ 5.
_____ _____ _____ 6.

Second Day:
_____ _____ _____ 1.
_____ _____ _____ 2.
_____ _____ _____ 3.
_____ _____ _____ 4.
_____ _____ _____ 5.
_____ _____ _____ 6.

Third Day:
_____ _____ _____ 1.
_____ _____ _____ 2.
_____ _____ _____ 3.
_____ _____ _____ 4.
_____ _____ _____ 5.
_____ _____ _____ 6.

Fourth Day:
_____ _____ _____ 1.
_____ _____ _____ 2.
_____ _____ _____ 3.
_____ _____ _____ 4.
_____ _____ _____ 5.
_____ _____ _____ 6.

3. In the first space before each of your log entries, place an "I" by those where you and the other person have an interdependent relationship; that is, each of you affects the other. This is in contrast to a dependent relationship where only one is affected by the other; perhaps a student-teacher relationship.

4. In the second space before each of your log entries, place an "E" by those in which there was actually an "expressed struggle;" that is, you and the other person had a conversation or discussion about the issue. Sometimes we are upset with another person's actions, but don't say anything, in which case, it's not really a conflict.

5. Use the third space to rank order from most intense to least intense, all of those situations that have both an "I" and an "E" in front of them.

Questions:

1. How do the situations that have both the I and E in front of them differ from the situations that don't?

2. What factors influence the level of intensity of the struggle among your situations?

3. What difference does it make in how you might behave that the situations without an "I" in front of them (aren't interdependent relationships) are not regarded to be interpersonal conflicts?

4. What difference does it make in how you might behave that the situations without an "E" in front of them (lack expressed struggle) are not regarded to be interpersonal conflicts

EXERCISE 8.2   IDENTIFYING GOALS IN CONFLICT SITUATIONS

Purpose:
1. To help you learn to identify goals in conflict situations.
2. To help you understand how the perception of different goals leads to conflict.

Directions:
1. Make a list of the conflicts you have been involved in during the last week or so (these can be little conflicts like deciding where to go to eat, what movie to see, etc.).
2. Identify what your goals were in each conflict.
3. Write down the goals the other person(s) had.

Participants	Your goals	Other person's goals	How the conflict was acted out
1.			
2.			
3.			
4.			

Questions:
1. How clear were you about your goals at the time of the conflict and how did that affect the conflict?

2. How well did you understand the other person's goals at the time of the conflict and how did that affect the conflict?

3. To what degree did the level of difference between your goal and the other person's affect the intensity of the conflict?

EXERCISE 8.3   CONFLICT AND DIVERSITY

Purpose:
1. To help you recognize cultural differences in conflict situations.

Directions:
1. Watch a movie or a television show in which different cultures are represented (gender, age, nationality, etc.); for example, *Survivor, Apprentice, Lost, MTV's Road Rules, Joy Luck Club, Black Rain, Crash,* and *Finding Forrester.*
2. Observe the behavior of the actors/participants in conflict situations.
3. Using the information in Chapter 8 in the text, record any differences in behavior that you notice.

Name the show: _____

Describe the participants: _____

_____

_____

_____

Describe the conflict situation: _____

_____

_____

_____

Describe the gender differences: (if applicable) _____

_____

_____

_____

Describe the cultural differences: (if applicable) _____

_____

_____

_____

Questions:

1. Do you think the conflict you observed was a true representation of "typical" conflict behavior for the cultures involved? Why or why not?

2. How did the factors of diversity affect the conflict?

3. How did the conflict behaviors compare to the information in Chapter 8 of your text?

4. What advice would you give the participants based on what you've learned in this class to help them improve the management of their conflict?

5. What lessons did you learn about intercultural conflict from watching this conflict?

EXERCISE 8.4   CATEGORIZING CONFLICT TYPES

Purpose:
1. To help you learn the differences between the three types of conflict--pseudo conflict, simple conflict, and ego conflict.
2. To learn to recognize the communication behaviors used in each conflict type.

Directions:
1. For each type of conflict, give an example from your experiences or observations of other people in conflict.
2. Describe the communication behaviors for each type of conflict that led you to choose the conflict to represent each type.

PSEUDO CONFLICT:

Description of a pseudo conflict: _____

_____

_____

Communication behaviors used by each participant: _____

_____

_____

Outcome of the conflict: _____

_____

_____

SIMPLE CONFLICT:

Description of a simple conflict: _____

_____

_____

Communication behaviors used by each participant: _____

_____

_____

Outcome of the conflict: _____

_____

_____

EGO CONFLICT:
Description of an ego conflict: _____

_____

_____

Communication behaviors used by each participant: _____

_____

_____

Outcome of the conflict: _____

_____

_____

Questions:

1.   Which type of conflict was most difficult for you to find an example of?

2.   Which type of conflict do you have most in your interpersonal relationships?

3.   How did the communication behaviors affect the outcome of the conflicts?

4.   What could have been done differently to change the outcome (if the outcome was not satisfactory to the participants)?

EXERCISE 8.5   MOVING THROUGH THE STAGES OF CONFLICT

Purpose:
1. To help you recognize how conflict moves through the stages of prior conditions, frustration awareness, active, resolution, and follow up stages.
2. To become aware of the communication behaviors used during each stage.

Directions:
1. Think about a recent conflict that you have had or are having and trace its development through the stages of conflict escalation.
2. If it is a conflict that hasn't been resolved, plot the evolution of the conflict to its current stage and consider some possible solutions for the conflict.
3. Identify the communication behaviors you and your partner used in each stage.

---

1. Source: Prior Conditions: What was the source of the conflict?   What communication behaviors were used?

2. Beginning: Frustration Awareness: When and how did you become aware of the conflict? What communication behaviors were used?

3. Middle: Active Conflict: How long did the actual interaction about the issues last (or is lasting)? What communication behaviors occurred during this time? How did communication change?

4. End: Resolution: Is there a solution? If so, what is it? If not, what are some ways the conflict could be managed? What communication behaviors were used?

5. Aftermath follow up: What communication behaviors were used to reach this point? In what ways has communication been affected?

EXERCISE 8.6   CONFLICT MANAGEMENT STYLES IN CONFLICT

Purpose:
1. To examine the nature of the five conflict management styles.
2. To see how conflict management styles interact with each other.

Directions:
1. Identify a.) a close friend of the same sex. b.) a close friend of the opposite sex. c.) a parent or other relative with whom you occasionally have conflicts.
2. Go through the lists of behaviors and attitudes. Check off those that are most commonly exhibited by you, and then for the others.

Conflict Styles	**You**	**Same Sex Friend**	**Opposite Sex Friend**	**Parent**
Avoidance				
Tries to side-step confrontations	_____	_____	_____	_____
Generally uncomfortable dealing with conflict	_____	_____	_____	_____
Things just not worth getting into a fight about	_____	_____	_____	_____
Has little concern for self or partner's goals	_____	_____	_____	_____
Accommodation				
Primarily concerned with partner's feelings	_____	_____	_____	_____
Easily gives in to the demands of others	_____	_____	_____	_____
Afraid conflict will offend, wants to be liked	_____	_____	_____	_____
Puts partner's goals above their own.	_____	_____	_____	_____
Competition				
Usually firm in pursuing own goals	_____	_____	_____	_____
Wants to win at all costs	_____	_____	_____	_____
Tends to dominate and control the discussion	_____	_____	_____	_____
Puts own goals above the partner's goals	_____	_____	_____	_____

Conflict Styles	You	Same Sex Friend	Opposite Sex Friend	Parent
Compromise				
Willing to give up some points to win some	_____	_____	_____	_____
Looks for solutions that split the difference	_____	_____	_____	_____
Looks for a middle ground	_____	_____	_____	_____
Both parties must accept some loses and gains	_____	_____	_____	_____
Collaboration				
Approaches conflicts as problems to be solved	_____	_____	_____	_____
Works with the partner to find a solution	_____	_____	_____	_____
Wants open, direct discussion of the issues	_____	_____	_____	_____
Concern for both parties getting their way	_____	_____	_____	_____

Questions

1.   a. Which person(s) do you have the most difficulty managing conflicts?

   b. In what ways do you and your partner's conflict management styles hamper effective conflict management?

2.   a. Which person(s) do you have the most success managing conflict?

   b. In what ways do you and your partner's conflict management styles assist effective conflict management?

3.   What changes could you and the others make to improve your management of conflict in your relationship?

EXERCISE 8.7   DESCRIBING YOUR CONFLICTS

Purpose:
1.   To learn to look at both sides of a conflict situation.

Directions:
1.   During the next week, choose three conflicts to analyze. These conflicts do not have to be major conflicts, but simply situations where you and another person are preventing one or the other from achieving a goal.
2.   Describe the conflict in terms of who it was with, what it was about, when it occurred, what the outcome was, how it was resolved, etc.
3.   Describe your perspective--what you saw as the problem and the cause, how you behaved, how you felt, how you think the other person behaved.
4.   Try to decenter and describe the conflict from the other person's perspective, by looking at what they would say the problem was, what the cause was, how they think you behaved, how they felt, how they would describe their behavior.

CONFLICT #1

Describe the conflict: _____

_____

_____

Give your perspective of the conflict: _____

_____

_____

Give your interpretation of the other person's perspective: _____

_____

_____

Optional: Obtain the other person's actual perception: _____

_____

_____

Identify what you discovered by comparing perspectives: _____

_____

_____

CONFLICT #2

Describe the conflict: _____

_____

_____

Give your perspective of the conflict: _____

_____

_____

Give your interpretation of the other person's perspective: _____

_____

_____

Optional: Obtain the other person's actual perception: _____

_____

_____

Identify what you discovered by comparing perspectives: _____

_____

_____

CONFLICT #3

Describe the conflict: _____

_____

_____

Give your perspective of the conflict: _____

_____

_____

Give your interpretation of the other person's perspective: _____

_____

_____

Optional: Obtain the other person's actual perception: _____

_____

_____

Identify what you discovered by comparing perspectives: _____

_____

_____

Questions:
1. What is the relationship between the effectiveness in which the conflict was managed and your ability to describe the other person's perspective?

2. If you obtained the actual perspectives of the other people, to what degree did your accuracy or inaccuracy relate to the management of the conflict?

EXERCISE 8.8   IDENTIFYING GOALS

Purpose:
1.   To learn to focus your conflicts on wants and needs (goals).
2.   To consider the wants and needs of others.

Directions:
1.   If possible use two current, on-going, important conflicts.
2.   Determine what you want and what you need (must get) in each situation.
3.   Identify what you think the other person wants and needs.

CONFLICT #1

Describe the conflict: _____

_____

_____

What I **WANT** out of this situation is: _____

_____

What I **NEED** (must get) out of this situation is: _____

_____

I believe the other person **WANTS**: _____

_____

I believe the other person **NEEDS** (must get): _____

_____

I believe this is what my partner wants and needs because:_____

_____

CONFLICT #2

Describe the conflict: _____

_____

_____

What I **WANT** out of this situation is: _____

_____

(Conflict # 2 Continued)

What I **NEED** (must get) out of this situation is: _____

_____

I believe the other person **WANTS**: _____

_____

I believe the other person **NEEDS** (must get): _____

_____

I believe this is what my partner wants and needs because:_____

_____

Questions:

1. How might your wants be interfering with managing the conflicts?

2. Your needs should be the minimum you need and still feel satisfied. How might you change the needs you've listed to further minimize them?

3. In what ways are your needs and the other people's needs in conflict?

4. In what ways do your needs overlap with the other people's needs?

5. What could be done to allow both you and the other people to both get their needs satisfied?

EXERCISE 8.9   ANALYZING AND MANAGING YOUR CONFLICTS

Purpose:
1. To apply the steps for managing conflict to your experiences.

Directions:
1. For each of the conflict analyses below, provide the requested information and answer the follow-up questions.

Managing Emotions:
Think of an interpersonal conflict in which you got upset, angry, or highly emotional during the interaction.

1. Were you aware that you were becoming emotional? If so, how could this help you? If not, why not?

2. What caused you to become emotional? Would the same factors cause you to get emotional again? How can you offset the impact of these causes?

3. To what degree did name-calling, personal attacks, or emotional overstatements arouse your emotions? How can you reduce that impact?

4. How would planning your message, selecting a mutually acceptable time to discuss, and the use of self-talk have helped you manage your emotions?

Managing Information: Think about an interpersonal conflict you experienced in which there was a lot of difficulty in reaching understanding and in sharing information.

1. At the time, how aware were you of the events that created the conflict? What impact did your level of awareness have on managing the conflict?

2. How well did you describe the events that lead to the conflict to your partner? What else might you have said or not said?

3. To what degree did you own your statements by using descriptive "I" language, such as, "I feel really upset..." or "What I really want is..."? How do such statements affect conflict management?

4. How effectively did you listen to the other person? How effectively did the other person seem to listen?

Managing Goals: Think about an <u>on-going</u> conflict in which you and the other person's goals really seemed at odds with one another.

1. What were your goals?

2. What were your partner's goals?

3. How effectively did you communicate your goals to your partner?

4. How well did you listen to your partner state his or her goals?

5. How open were you to helping your partner achieve his or her goals?

Managing the Problem: Use the conflict just discussed above on managing goals.

1. Define the problem from both points of view.

2. Analyze the problem. What are the symptoms, effects, and obstacles? What other information is needed?

3. Determine you and your partner's goals. (Answers to 1 and 2 from managing goals).

4. Generate multiple possible solutions. Be creative and brainstorm.

5. Select the best solution; how well does it fulfill the goals of you and your partner?

EXERCISE 8.10   DEALING WITH PRICKLY PEOPLE

Purpose:

1. To understand and apply the strategies for managing conflict with prickly people (people who rub you the wrong way).

Directions:

1. Think about a recent or particularly memorable interpersonal conflict that you have had with a prickly person (this can be a conflict that is currently occurring) and describe it below:

    Conflict Description (what are the issues, who is the other person, why have you had difficulty with this person):

2. Evaluate that interaction in terms of which strategies occurred and explain how you the strategies you didn't use might have been applied to this conflict.

Gone to the Balcony (took a time out to cool off)

Step to the Side (switched from arguing to asking questions and listening)

Changed the Frame (considered the issue from someone else's perspective)

Built a Golden Bridge (helped the other person save face while agreeing to my side)

Made it Hard to Say No (provided information to understand the benefits of your position)

Interpersonal Conflict	Interdependent
Simple Conflict	Pseudo Conflict
Instrumental Conflict	Ego Conflict
Flaming	Expressive Conflict
Destructive Conflict	Conflict Style
Constructive Conflict	Demand-Withdrawal Pattern of Conflict Management

Dependent on each other; one person's actions affect the other person.	Expressed struggle that occurs when people cannot agree on a way to meet their needs or goals.
Conflict triggered by a lack of understanding and miscommunication.	Conflict that stems from different ideas, definitions, perceptions, or goals.
Conflict in which the original issue is ignored as partners attack each other's self esteem.	Conflict that centers on achieving a particular goal or task and less on relational issues.
Conflict that focuses on issues about the quality of the relationship and managing interpersonal tension and hostility.	Sending an overly negative online message that personally attacks another person.
The consistent pattern or approach you use to manage disagreement with others.	Conflict that dismantles relationships rather than strengthens relationships.
Pattern in which one person makes a demand and the other person avoids conflict by changing the subject or walking away.	Conflict that helps build new insights and establishes new patterns in a relationship.

Avoidance	Accommodation
Competition	Compromise
Collaboration	Gunny Sacking
But Message	"I" Language
Face	

Conflict management style that involves giving in to the demands of others.	Conflict management style that involves backing off and trying to side-step conflict.
Conflict management style that attempts to find the middle ground in a conflict.	Conflict management style that stresses winning a conflict at the expense of the other person involved.
Dredging up old problems and issues from the past to use against your partner.	Conflict management style that uses other-oriented strategies to achieve a positive solution for all involved.
Statements that use the word "*I*" to express how a speaker is feeling.	Statement using the word *but* that may communicate that whatever you've said prior to *but* is not really true.
	Self-image or self-respect that you and your partner seek to maintain

CHAPTER 9
UNDERSTANDING INTERPERSONAL RELATIONSHIPS

OBJECTIVES

After studying this chapter in the text, *Interpersonal Communication: Relating to Others*, and completing the exercises in this section of the study guide, you should understand:

1. The meaning of the term interpersonal relationship.
2. The difference between a relationship of circumstance and a relationship of choice.
3. Short term initial attraction and long term maintenance attraction.
4. The elements that contribute to short term initial attraction.
5. The elements that contribute to both short term initial attraction and long-term maintenance attraction.
6. The types of power relationships.
6. The five bases of interpersonal power.
7. How power is negotiated in relationships.
8. How friendships change during our lifetimes.
9. The triangular theory of love.
10. The six types of love.
11. The types of relationships found in families.

STUDY QUESTIONS

You should be able to answer the following questions:

1. Define interpersonal relationships and discuss its components?
2. How are relationships of circumstance and relationships of choice different?
3. What is the difference between short-term initial attraction and long-term maintenance attraction?
4. Explain the factors that lead to short-term initial attraction.
5. Discuss the factors that contribute to both short-term initial and long-term maintenance attraction.
6. Explain the five principles of power.
7. Define the five types of power relationships?
8. What are the five types of power found in relationships?
9. How is power negotiated in relationships?
10. Why are friendships important to us throughout our lives?
11. Explain the triangular theory of love.
12. Describe four types of married couples.

EXERCISE 9.1   UNDERSTANDING INTERPERSONAL RELATIONSHIPS

Purpose:
1. To understand the four elements that constitute the definition of an interpersonal relationship.
2. To appreciate how your interpersonal relationships differ.

Directions:
1. Write down the first names of five people that you know who vary in their relationship with you including casual friends, best friends, family members, etc.
2. Rate each relationship in terms of the four elements of the definition of interpersonal relationships using the following scale :

     O = None   1 = Some   2 = A fair amout   3 = Great deal

Four Elements Constituting the Definition of Interpersonal Relationships

     Degree of **Shared Perception** (both see relationship similarly)

     Degree of **Ongoing Connection** (process, relational development)

     Amount of **Relational Expectations** (what you expect from your)

     Degree of **Interpersonal Intimacy** (mutual confirmation and acceptance of each other's self)

FIRST NAMES	Shared Perception	Ongoing Connection	Relational Expecations	Interpersonal Intimacy
1. _____	_____	_____	_____	_____
2. _____	_____	_____	_____	_____
3. _____	_____	_____	_____	_____
4. _____	_____	_____	_____	_____
5. _____	_____	_____	_____	_____

Questions:
1. According to the four dimensions, how do the relationships differ?

2. According to the four dimensions, how are the relationships similar?

3. In what ways do the relationships differ that aren't reflected in the four dimensions?

EXERCISE 9.2   QUALITIES OF INTIMACY

Purpose:
1. To evaluate your own conception of intimacy and how it is reflected in your relationships.

Directions:
1. In the space provided, brainstorm a list of qualities you associate with A) an intimate friendship) and B) an intimate lover relationship (husband/wife).

**Qualities you associate with
friendships you consider intimate**

**Qualities you associate with lover
relationships (including married couples)**

_____   _____

_____   _____

_____   _____

_____   _____

_____   _____

_____   _____

_____   _____

Questions:
1. What differences are there between the two lists?

2. Why were certain qualities associated with one relationship and not the other?

3. How well do your current relationships match up to these qualities?

EXERCISE 9.3   OBSERVING OTHERS

Purpose:
1. To become aware of the characteristics you consider attractive and repulsive.
2. To determine the characteristics of others that would lead you to pursue relationships.

Directions:
1. Put yourself in situations where you can observe five different people who you do not know interacting with other people (choose people of different races, cultures, ages, or occupations).
2. Make a list of the qualities each person has that are attractive to you.
3. Make a list of the qualities each person has that are unattractive to you.
4. Indicate which of the people you would like to get to know better, if you had the chance. (Or indicate with which of the people you did start a conversation.)

PERSON#	ATTRACTIVE QUALITIES	UNATTRACTIVE QUALITIES	REASON TO PURSUE

EXERCISE 9.4   **SHORT TERM INITIAL ATTRACTION AND
LONG-TERM MAINTENANCE ATTRACTION**

Purpose:
1.   To determine the reasons you started your best friend relationship.
2.   To understand the reasons you have maintained the friendship.

Directions:
1.   Think of your best same-sex friend and your best opposite-sex friend.
2.   List the reasons you became friends with these people.
3.   List the reasons you have maintained friendships with these people.

Same Sex Friend	Initial reasons for the relationship	Current reasons for the relationship

Opposite Sex Friend	Initial reasons for the relationship	Current reasons for the relationship

Questions:
1.   How are the reasons for each of your best friends different? Similar?

2.   Which initial reasons for the same-sex friendship are still reasons you are friends?

3.   Which initial reasons for the opposite-sex friendship are still reasons you are friends?

EXERCISE 9.5   DISCOVERING SIMILARITIES AND DIFFERENCES

Purpose:
1. To discover how similarities and differences in personality, values, cultural background, personal experiences, attitudes, and interests impact relationships.

Directions:
1. Think of the closest relationship you have (best friend, spouse, relative).
2. List the similarities between you and the other person in each category below.
3. List the differences between you and the other person in each category below.

CATEGORIES	SIMILARITIES	DIFFERENCES
Personality		
Values		
Cultural background		
Personal experiences		
Attitudes		
Interests		

Questions:
1. How do the similarities affect your relationship?

2. To what degree to the differences create attraction? Conflict?

EXERCISE 9.6 EVALUATING INTERPERSONAL NEEDS

Purpose:
1. To become aware of your need to be included, to be controlled, and to be liked/accepted.
2. To become aware of your need to include others (item 1), to be included by others (item 2), to control others and make decisions (item 3), to have other's make decisions (item 4), to like others (item 5), and to be like by others (item 6).
3. To investigate the compatibility of your needs with the needs of others.
4. To investigate the affect of compatibility of needs on the level of closeness.

Directions:
1. Evaluate your level of interpersonal needs for each of the following questions by putting your first initial above the number which corresponds to your rating.
2. Ask two close friends to place their first initial below the number on each scale to indicate how much each item applies to them.
3. Compare your rating with those of your friends.

---

1. How much do you like to include others in the activities you do?

   Very little   **1-----2-----3-----4-----5-----6-----7-----8-----9-----10**   **A great deal**

2. How much do you like to be included by others in activities they are doing?

   Very little   **1-----2-----3-----4-----5-----6-----7-----8-----9-----10**   **A great deal**

3. How much do you like to take responsibility for decision-making?

   Very little   **1-----2-----3-----4-----5-----6-----7-----8-----9-----10**   **A great deal**

4. How much do you like to let others make decisions for you?

   Very little   **1-----2-----3-----4-----5-----6-----7-----8-----9-----10**   **A great deal**

5. How much do you feel a need to be accepted and loved by others?

   Very little   **1-----2-----3-----4-----5-----6-----7-----8-----9-----10**   **A great deal**

6. How much do you feel a need to accept others and to give love to others?

   Very little   **1-----2-----3-----4-----5-----6-----7-----8-----9-----10**   **A great deal**

Questions:
1. In what areas are your needs similar to your friends' needs?

2. In what areas are your needs complementary to your friends' needs?

Questions Continued:

3. Which matching or differing areas cause difficulties in the relationship, e.g., you both want to make decisions, one wants lots of affection, and the other doesn't like to give affection?

Repeat this exercise by choosing two people you know on a casual basis (a classmate, co-worker). Follow the same instructions as above.

---

1. How much do you like to include others in the activities you do?

    Very little   1-----2-----3-----4-----5-----6-----7-----8-----9-----10   A great deal

2. How much do you like to be included by others in activities they are doing?

    Very little   1-----2-----3-----4-----5-----6-----7-----8-----9-----10   A great deal

3. How much do you like to take responsibility for decision-making?

    Very little   1-----2-----3-----4-----5-----6-----7-----8-----9-----10   A great deal

4. How much do you like to let others make decisions for you?

    Very little   1-----2-----3-----4-----5-----6-----7-----8-----9-----10   A great deal

5. How much do you feel a need to be accepted and loved by others?

    Very little   1-----2-----3-----4-----5-----6-----7-----8-----9-----10   A great deal

6. How much do you feel a need to accept others and to give love to others?

    Very little   1-----2-----3-----4-----5-----6-----7-----8-----9-----10   A great deal

---

Questions:

1. In what areas are your needs similar to your friends' needs?

2. In what areas are your needs complementary to your friends' needs?

3. Which matching or differing areas cause difficulties in the relationship, e.g., you both want to make decisions, one wants lots of affection, and the other doesn't like to give affection?

4. How do similar or complementary needs affect the level of your relationships?

EXERCISE 9.7 **DISCOVERING YOUR OWN LOVE PROFILE**

Purpose:
1. To become aware of your attitude toward "love."
2. To compare your attitude toward love with those of others

Directions:
1. On a separate piece of paper, write out 1 to 24 and then record your responses to each item using the following five point scale:

   1 = Strongly   **2 = Disagree**   **3 = Neutral**   **4 = Agree**   **5 = Strongly**
        Disagree   **Agree**

2. Have one or two friends or classmates write out and record their responses to the items.

_____1. You cannot love unless you have first had a caring relationship for a while.

_____2. The best kind of love grows out of a long friendship.

_____3. Kissing, cuddling, and sex should not be rushed into; they will happen naturally when intimacy has grown.

_____4. Love is really deep friendship, not a mysterious, mystical emotion.

_____5. I believe that "love at first sight" is possible.

_____6. We kissed each other soon after we met because we both wanted to.

_____7. Usually the first thing that attracts my attention to a person is a pleasing appearance.

_____8. Strong physical attraction is one of the best things about being in love.

_____9. When things are not going right with us, my stomach gets upset.

_____10. Once when I thought a love affair was over, I saw him or her again and the old feelings came surging back.

_____11. If my partner ignores me for a while, I sometimes do really stupid things to try to get his or her attention.

_____12. When my partner does not pay attention to me, I feel sick all over.

_____13. I try to use my own strength to help my partner through difficult times, even when he or she is behaving foolishly.

_____14. I am usually willing to sacrifice my own wishes in favor of my partner's.

_____15. If my partner had a baby by someone else, I would want to raise it and care for it as if it were my own.

_____16. I would rather break up with my partner than stand in his or her way.

_____17. For practical reasons, I would consider what he or she is going to become before I commit myself.

_____18. You should plan your life before choosing a partner.

_____19. A main consideration is choosing a partner is how he or she reflects on my family.

_____20. I would not date anyone that I would not want to fall in love with.

_____21. At least once I had to plan carefully to keep two of my lovers from finding out about each other.

_____22. I can get over love affairs pretty easily and quickly.

_____23. My partner would get upset if he or she knew some of the things I have done with other people.

_____24. What he or she does not know about me will not hurt my partner.

Scoring:

Add items 1-4 and divide by 4 for a friendship factor (storge) score.
Add items 5-8 and divide by 4 for the passionate factor (eros) score.
Add items 9-12 and divide by 4 for the possessive factor (mania) score.
Add items 13-16 and divide by 4 for the selflessness factor (agape) score.
Add items 17-20 and divide by 4 for the practical factor (pragma) score.
Add items 21-14 and divide by 4 for the game-playing factor (ludis) score.

Questions:

1. In looking at the types of love you scored strongest on, what does this probably mean for the type of romantic relationship you would find most satisfying?

2. What are the similarities and differences between you and the other people who completed the items? Are you very compatible?

3. Discuss the areas that you and the other people differ and provide an answer for why you probably have these differences.

EXERCISE 9.8   WATCHING FOR POWER CUES

<u>**Purpose:**</u>
1.   To learn to recognize cues that indicates power during communication interactions.
2.   To assess your own use of power cues.

<u>**Directions:**</u>
1.   Observe three different pairs of friends and/or family members engaged in a debate or an argument.
2.   List any communication behaviors you observed which reflected an attempt to gain power or control over the other.
3.   List any communication behaviors you observed which reflected submission or lack of power (for example, looking down, talking meekly, giving in to the other)

POWERFUL CUES	**POWERLESS CUES**

COUPLE #1

COUPLE #2

COUPLE #3

Questions:

1. Which "powerful" cues did people use most often?

2. Which "powerless" cues did people use most often?

3. To what degree were each of the interactants affected by their partner's use of powerful cues?

4. To what extent were each of the interactants affected by their partner's use of powerless cues?

5. Which powerful or powerless cues are typical of your own behavior toward other people?

6. Which powerful cues do you find most difficult to display? Why? How could you overcome this?

EXERCISE 9.9   CHECKING POWER BALANCE

Purpose:
1. To become aware of your perception of power in a conflict situation.

Directions:
1. Think of a conflict in which you are currently involved.
2. Rate your perception of your own power and the power of your partner in relation to the conflict.
3. If possible, give your partner a copy of the survey so you can compare perceptions.

Fill out the survey below according to the following:
Put a "3" in the space if person is strong in this type of power with the partner
Put a "2" in the space if the person has medium strength in this type of power with the partner
Put a "1" in the space if the person has low strength or doesn't have this type of power with the partner

---

Self		*Other*
_____	Legitimate Power (Position)	_____
_____	Referent Power (Reputation)	_____
_____	Coercive Power (Ability to Punish)	_____
_____	Reward Power (Resource Control)	_____
_____	Expert Power (Knowledge and Skill)	_____
_____	Compliance Gaining Skills	_____
_____	**TOTALS**	_____

Scoring: If your total power score and that of your partner are within 4 points of each other, you are in an equal-power situation. A difference greater than 4 points suggests an unequal balance of power.

Ask your partner to fill out the copy of the survey on the next page (You will need to briefly explain each type of power to your partner). Compare your perceptions of power in this conflict situation.

Please fill out the survey below according to the following:

Put a "3" in the space if person is strong in this type of power with the partner

Put a "2" in the space if the person has medium strength in this type of power with the partner

Put a "1" in the space if the person has low strength or doesn't have this type of power with the partner

Self		_Other_
_____	Legitimate Power (Position)	_____
_____	Referent Power (Reputation)	_____
_____	Coercive Power (Ability to Punish)	_____
_____	Reward Power (Resource Control)	_____
_____	Expert Power (Knowledge and Skill)	_____
_____	Compliance Gaining Skills	_____
_____	**TOTALS**	_____

Questions:

1. If your total power score and that of your partner are within 4 points of each other, you are in an equal-power situation. A difference greater than 4 points suggests an unequal balance of power.

   A. How balanced is the power in your relationship?

   B. What is the major source of any power differences?

2. How is the power distribution contributing to the conflict situation?

3. What can you do to manage any power differences?

4. How has power changed in the relationship? How did this relate to the conflict?

EXERCISE 9.10   NEGOTIATING POWER IN RELATIONSHIPS

<u>**Purpose:**</u>
1.   To understand and practice negotiating power in relationships.

<u>**Directions:**</u>
1.   Think about a current relationship in which you are dissatisfied with the balance of power or how the other person is exercising power toward you.
2.   Complete the items drawn from the text.

A) Assess Needs
What needs are you expecting to be filled by this relationship?

What needs does you partner expect to be filled by this relationship?

B) Assess Need Fulfillment
How well is the relationship fulfilling your needs identified above?

How well is the relationship fulfilling the needs you identified for your partner?

C) Identify Need Based Conflicts and Tensions
What specific actions or events have occurred that reflect power problems?

What are your feelings about the way power is distributed in this relationship?

D) Directly Discuss Power Issues
What factors are restraining you from discussing the above issues?

How do you think your partner will react to your attempt to discuss this? What can you say to encourage an open discussion?

EXERCISE 9.11   FRIENDHIPS THROUGHOUT YOUR LIFE

Purpose:
1.   To appreciate the changes in relationships during different times in your life.

Directions:
1.   Provide the information requested under each of the categories below (for those relationship that extend over time, describe the relationship during the specified time period)

THE FIRST FRIEND/PLAYMATE YOU CAN REMEMBER   First name

A) What initially attracted you to this person?

B) How did you spend your time together?

C) To what degree did you feel this person really knew you?

D) What needs were met by this relationship?

E) What did you like most about this relationship?

F) What did you like least about this relationship?

YOUR CLOSEST FRIEND IN ELEMENTARY SCHOOL   First name:

A) What initially attracted you to this person?

B) How did you spend your time together?

C) To what degree did you feel this person really knew you?

D) What needs were met by this relationship?

E) What did you like most about this relationship?

F) What did you like least about this relationship?

YOUR CLOSEST FRIEND IN HIGH SCHOOL   First name: _____

A) What initially attracted you to this person?

B) How did you spend your time together?

C) To what degree did you feel this person really knew you?

D) What needs were met by this relationship?

E) What did you like most about this relationship?

F) What did you like least about this relationship?

YOUR CURRENT CLOSEST FRIEND   First name: _____

A) What initially attracted you to this person?

B) How did you spend your time together?

C) To what degree did you feel this person really knew you?

D) What needs were met by this relationship?

E) What did you like most about this relationship?

F) What did you like least about this relationship?

Questions:

1. How have your relationships changed over time?

2. What similarities are there among the relationships (if any)? Why?

EXERCISE 9.12   ADVERTISING FOR FRIENDSHIPS

Purpose:
1. To understand characteristics you look for in different types of friendships.

Directions:
1. Write "job-like" ads for filling the specific friendship vacancies listed below
2. Identify the qualities and communication behaviors you want in the other person.
3. Identify the qualities and communication behaviors you have to offer.
   Example: For a friend of the same sex, "Wanted: Male between 20 and 27 who likes jogging with conversation, likes talking about sports, doesn't feel the need to discuss emotions or relationships, talks in support of conservative political issues, likes joking around and teasing, and doesn't need to always be included."

Advertisement For A Friend Of The Same Sex

_____

_____

_____

_____

Advertisement For A Friend Of The Opposite Sex

_____

_____

_____

_____

Advertisement For An Intimate/Romantic/Lover Relationship

_____

_____

_____

_____

Advertisement For An Intergenerational Friend (someone at least 20 years older)

_____

_____

_____

_____

Questions:

1. How do the personal characteristics differ in your ads? Stay the same? Why?

2. What communication qualities/behaviors are similar? Different? Why?

3. What specific goals would you have for each type of friendship--escape loneliness, share experiences, give emotional support, talk, etc.?

4. On what basis did you decide what qualities to list for each advertisement?

5. The ads reflect your "expectations" about relationships. How might they affect your ability to initiate and form satisfying relationships?

6. The ads reflect qualities about you. What inferences about you might other people draw after examining your ads?

EXERCISE 9.13   FRIENDSHIPS WITH A DIFFERENCE

Purpose:
1. To assess the advantages and disadvantages of relationships with people who are different from us.
2. To appreciate intergenerational, intercultural, interracial, and cross-sex friendships.

Directions:
1. For each relationship type, either use an actual relationship you have had that fits the category, or imagine such a relationship as you identify and write down the advantages and disadvantages associated with such a relationship.

	Advantages	**Disadvantages**
Intergenerational Friendship (with someone of the same sex at least 30 years older than you)		
Intercultural Friendship (with someone your age and sex from another country with a different first language than you)		
Interracial Friendship (with someone of the same sex that is your age and of a different race than you)		
Cross-Sex Friendship (with someone of the opposite sex that is your age with no desires for the relationship to become romantic)		

<u>Questions:</u>

1. Which relationship would seem to be the easiest to form and maintain? Why?

2. Which relationship would be the most difficult to form and maintain? Why?

3. Overall, which outweighs the other, the advantages or the disadvantages? Why?

4. What common advantages were identified? Why do you suppose those are common to these types of relationships?

5. What relationship had the most unique collection of advantages and disadvantages? What makes that relationship so different?

EXERCISE 9.14   IDENTIFYING MARITAL ROLE EXPECTATIONS

Purpose:

1. To help you to identify the role behavior expectations you take into your relationships.
2. To determine whether your expectations are the same as or different than those of a significant person in your life.

Directions:

1. Indicate which of the behaviors listed on the questionnaire below are the primary responsibilities of the wife (W), the husband (H), or both (H/W).
2. Beside each response, state the reasons you responded as you did.

_____   Taking out the garbage.

_____   Writing thank-you notes.

_____   Initiating sexual activity.

_____   Balancing the checkbook.

_____   Changing diapers.

_____   Bringing home a paycheck.

_____   Disciplining the children.

_____   Doing the laundry.

_____   Planning for retirement.

_____   Cooking.

_____   Cleaning the bathrooms.

_____   Changing the oil in the car.

_____   Driving children to school.

_____   Mending clothes.

_____   Cleaning gutters on the house.

_____   Buying birthday presents for the parents.

Ask your spouse, person you are dating, or appropriate friend to fill out this questionnaire:

<u>Directions:</u>
1. Indicate which of the behaviors listed on the questionnaire below are the primary responsibilities of the wife (W), the husband (H), or both (H/W).
2. Beside each response, state the reasons you responded as you did.

_____ Taking out the garbage.

_____ Writing thank-you notes.

_____ Initiating sexual activity.

_____ Balancing the checkbook.

_____ Changing diapers.

_____ Bringing home a paycheck.

_____ Disciplining the children.

_____ Doing the laundry.

_____ Planning for retirement.

_____ Cooking.

_____ Cleaning the bathrooms.

_____ Changing the oil in the car.

_____ Driving children to school.

_____ Mending clothes.

_____ Cleaning gutters on the house.

_____ Buying birthday presents for the parents.

Questions:

1. On which items did your partner agree with you?

2. On which items did your partner disagree with you? Why do you think you have different ideas about these items?

3. If you were to live together, how would you handle the differences in your role expectations?

Interpersonal Relationship	Relationship
Relationship of Choice	Relationship of Circumstance
Interpersonal Attraction	Interpersonal Intimacy
Long-Term Maintenance Attraction	Short-Term Initial Attraction
Similarity	Physical Appearance
Proximity	Predicted Outcome Value (POV)

Connection we establish when we communicate with another person.	Perception shared by two people of an ongoing connection that results in the development of relational expectations and varies in interpersonal intimacy.
Interpersonal relationship that exists because of life circumstances (who your family members are, where you work, or study, and so on).	Interpersonal relationship you choose to initiate, maintain, and terminate.
Degree to which relational partners mutually accept and confirm each other's sense of self.	Degree to which you want to form or maintain an interpersonal relationship.
Degree to which you sense a potential for developing an interpersonal relationship.	Degree of liking or positive feelings that motivate us to maintain or escalate a relationship.
Nonverbal cues that allow us to assess relationship potential (POV).	Having comparable personalities; values, upbringing, personal experiences, attitudes, and interests.
Potential for a relationship to confirm our self image compared to its potential costs.	Physical nearness to another that promotes communication and thus attraction.

Reciprocation of Liking	Complementary Needs
Dependent Relationship	Interdependent Relationship
Complementary Relationship	Interpersonal Power
Competitive Symmetric Relationship	Symmetric Relationship
Parallel Relationship	Submissive Symmetric Relationship
Referent Power	Legitimate Power

Needs that match, each partner contributes something to the relationship that the other partner needs.	Liking those who like us.
Relationship in which each person has a similar amount of power over the other.	Relationship in which one partner has a greater need for the other to meet his or her needs.
Degree to which a person is able to influence his or her partner.	Relationship in which power is divided unevenly, with one partner dominating and the other person submitting
Relationship in which both partners attempt to have the same level of power.	Relationship in which both partners vie for control or dominance of the other.
Relationship in which neither partner wants to take control or make decisions.	Relationship in which power shifts back and forth between the partners depending on the situation.
Power that is based on respect for a person's position.	Power that comes from our attraction to another person, or the charisma a person possesses.

Reward Power	Expert Power
Compliance Gaining	Coercive Power
Triangular Theory Of Love	Ludis
Eros	Mania
Storge	Agape
Pragma	Independent Couples

Power based on a person's knowledge and experience.	Power based on a person's ability to satisfy our needs.
Power based on the use of sanctions or punishments to influence others.	Persuasive actions take to get others to comply with our goals.
Game-playing love based upon the enjoyment of another.	Theory that suggests that all loving relationships can be described according to three dimensions: intimacy, commitment, and passion.
Obsessive love driven by mutual needs.	Sexual, erotic love based upon the pursuit of physical beauty and pleasure.
Selfless love based upon giving of yourself for others.	Solid love found in friendships and family based on trust and caring.
Married partners who exhibit sharing and companionship and are psychologically interdependent but allow each individual space.	Practical love based upon mutual benefits.

Traditional Couples	Mixed Couples
Separate Couples	

Married couples in which the husband and wife each adopt a different perspective (traditional, independent, separate) on marriage	Married partners who are interdependent and who exhibit a lot of sharing and companionship.
	Married partners who support the notion of marriage and family but stress the individual over the couple.

CHAPTER 10
DEVELOPING INTERPERSONAL RELATIONSHIPS

OBJECTIVES

After studying this chapter in the text, *Interpersonal Communication: Relating to Others*, and completing the exercises in this section of the study guide, you should understand:

1. The five stages of relational escalation.
2. The five stages of relational de-escalation.
3. How social exchange theory and dialectical theory explain relational development.
4. The skills and strategies used primarily to initiate relationships.
5. The skills and strategies for both initiating and escalating relationships.
6. The skills and strategies for both escalating and maintaining relationships.

STUDY QUESTIONS

You should be able to answer the following questions:

1. What are the five stages of relational escalation?
2. What stages occur when an intimate relationship moves to dissolution?
3. What are post-intimacy relationships?
4. What is social exchange theory and how does it relate to relationship development?
5. Describe the tensions that exist in interpersonal relationships according to dialectical theory.
6. What are the specific skills used to start relationships?
7. What is an affinity seeking strategy?
8. What skills can be used both in initiating and escalating a relationship?
9. What skills can be used specifically to escalate and maintain relationships?

EXERCISE 10.1   CHARTING RELATIONAL DEVELOPMENT

Purpose:
1. To determine the movement of relationships through stages.
2. To understand how perceptual differences affect relational development.

Directions:
1. Think of an interpersonal relationship that you have had for at least a year.
2. Plot the development of that relationship from stage to stage over time.
3. Cover up your chart and ask your partner to fill out the second one.
4. Compare your perceptions of how the relationship has developed with your partner's perceptions.

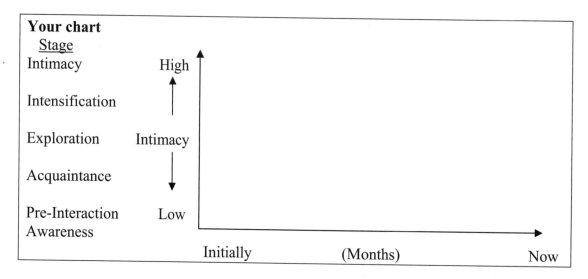

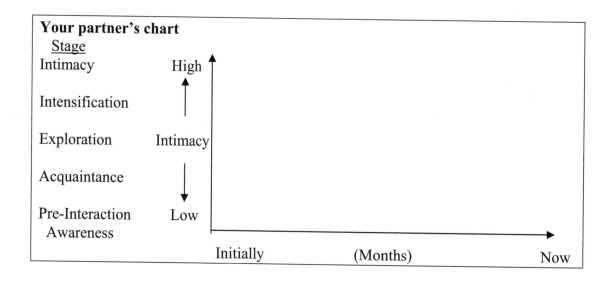

Questions:

1. What differences are there between your perceptions and your partner's perceptions?

2. Why do you think you and your partner may see your relationship in different stages of development at a particular time?

3. What can you tell from the charts about the nature of your relationship?

4. What specific turning points occurred in your relationship? (Usually identified with a strong change in intimacy or movement from one stage to another) Identify them as either causal or reflective turning points.

5. What explanation might there be for any time your relationship went back to a previous, less intimate stage?

EXERCISE 10.2   SOCIAL EXCHANGE ANALYSIS

Purpose:
1.   To analyze and compare relationships using social exchange principles.

Directions:
1.   Identify three relationships of choice that you currently have. Choose relationships that vary in terms of their level of intimacy.
2.   Rate each relationship on each of the social exchange components using the scales provided.

	Relationship 1	Relationship 2	Relationship 3
Current rewards provided by the relationship (0 to 10)	_____	_____	_____
Rewards you expect from this type of relationship (0 to 10)	_____	_____	_____
Current costs of the the relationship (0 to 10)	_____	_____	_____
Costs you expect in this type of relationship (0 to 10)	_____	_____	_____
Cumulative rewards minus costs (total -100 to +100)	_____	_____	_____
Forecasted rewards minus costs (total -100 to +100)	_____	_____	_____
Current level of satisfaction with the relationship (0 to 10)	_____	_____	_____

Questions
1.   Which relationship would social exchange theory predict is your best? How does this compare to your actually feelings about the relationships?

2.   How does your level of satisfaction compare to the various social exchange qualities? Which seems to relate the strongest to your satisfaction?

3.   Which of the qualities is easiest to calculate and which is the hardest? Why?

EXERCISE 10.3   ANALYZING TURNING POINTS AND DIALECTICAL TENSIONS

Purpose:
1. To analyze changes in a relationship according to dialectical tensions theory.

Directions:
1. Consider a relationship that you have had for some time that has gone through lots of changes (it can even be with your parents).
2. Briefly describe the "turning points" where the relationship significantly changed.
3. Identify which, if any, of the three pairs of dialectical tensions changed at each turning point—indicating whether the relationship became more connected, more autonomous, more predictable, more unpredictable (novel), more open, or more closed.

	ASSOCIATED CHANGE		
TURNING POINT	More connected or autonomous	More predictable or novel	More open or closed
1. _____ _____	_____	_____	_____
2. _____ _____	_____	_____	_____
3. _____ _____	_____	_____	_____
4. _____ _____	_____	_____	_____
5. _____ _____	_____	_____	_____
6. _____ _____	_____	_____	_____
7. _____ _____	_____	_____	_____
8. _____ _____	_____	_____	_____

Questions

1. What dialectical tension was **most** prevalent in your turning points? Why do you suppose this is?

2. What dialectical tension was **least** prevalent in your turning points? Why do you suppose this is?

3. Do you have some turning points where no changes occurred in the dialectical tensions? What does this reveal about what was changing in the relationship?

4. To what degree did some conflict occur as you attempted to resolve the tensions associated with each turning point?

5. If possible, ask your partner so share his or her perspective on each of the turning points and associated tensions? How similar or different are your perspectives and why?

6. Turning points and resolving tensions often involve "relational talk" where you and your partner discuss your views of the relationship. Which of your turning points involved relational talk and which didn't? How did that affect the process?

EXERCISE 10.4   PERCEIVING RELATIONSHIPS

Purpose:
1.   To understand how perceptions within a relationship differ.

Directions:
1.   Find a friend who is willing to do this exercise with you.
2.   Each of you is to write down answers to the following questions without discussing the questions or your responses until you have both written all your responses:
    a. Describe your perception of the relationship you have with each other.
    b. Describe how you think your partner will describe the relationship.
    c. Describe what you think your friend will say is your perception of the relationship.
3.   Compare your responses as you complete the questions.

Your Responses:

1. Your perception of the relationship.
2. How do you think your friend will describe the relationship?
3. What do you think your friend will say is your perception of the relationship?

Turn the page over and have your friend fill in the appropriate information or simply have your friend respond to the questions on a separate piece of paper.

Your Friend's Responses:

1. Your perception of the relationship.
2. What do you think your friend's perception of the relationship is?
3. What do you think your friend will say is your perception of the relationship?

Questions to answer after completing the exercise:

1. What similarities are there in your individual perceptions of the relationship?

2. What differences are there in your individual perceptions of the relationship?

3. How closely were each of you able to predict the other's perception of the relationship? (Compare your response to #1 to your partner's response to #2; and your partner's #1 to your #2). Who was more accurate? Why?

4. What does the degree of similarity or difference in all three responses suggest about the nature of your relationship?

EXERCISE 10.5   INITIATING RELATIONSHIPS

Purpose:
1. To practice some of the strategies provided in the text for initiating relationships.

Directions:
1. Study the strategies listed in the text for initiating relationships: observe and act on approachability cues, identify and use conversations starters, follow initiation norms, ask questions, and don't expect too much; PLUS communicate and cultivate attraction, be open and self-disclose appropriately, gather information to reduce uncertainty, monitor your perceptions, listen actively and respond confirmingly, and social decenter and adopt an other-oriented perspective.
2. Initiate a conversation with two different people over the next few days when you find yourself in an appropriate social situation where there are people you don't know (e.g. in the dining hall at meal time, at a party, sitting among a group in the student union). Don't put yourself in a situation that is overly uncomfortable or risky.
3. Try to choose two very different people, one who are similar to you (age, race, sex, nationality), and one who is different from you (age, race, sex, nationality).
4. Apply the strategies covered in the text and try to maintain a conversation for at least five minutes.

Questions:

1. How comfortable did you feel approaching the other people?

2. What things helped reduce your anxiety?

3. What else could you do to reduce your anxiety?

4. Which interaction was easier to initiate and maintain? Why?

5. What strategies did you use your initiations?

6. How effective were they in helping you initiate and continue the conversation?

7. What strategies might you have used that you didn't? How would they have helped?

EXERCISE 10.6   SINGING ABOUT RELATIONSHIPS

Purpose:
1. To familiarize you with some of the popular sentiments concerning interpersonal relationships as they are expressed in song.
2. To stimulate you to consider the significant concepts and theories in interpersonal relationships by relating them to familiar songs.

Directions:
1. Identify four songs that do any of the following:
   a) expresses a sentiment that provides insight into interpersonal relationships.
   b) illustrates an important interpersonal relationship concept or theory .
   c) illustrates a popular relational problem or difficulty.
   d) illustrates a method for dealing with relationship problems or difficulties.

NAME OF THE SONG and ARTIST	EXPLANATION FOR HOW IT RELATES TO INTERPERSONAL RELATIONSHIPS
1.	
2.	
3.	
4.	

Questions:

1. In general, what is your sense of how common the theme of interpersonal relationships is in contemporary songs? Explain.

2. Which relational issues or themes appear to be most common?

3. What contradictions did you find between what the songs have to say about relationships compared to the text?

EXERCISE 10.7   WATCHING FRIENDSHIPS ON TV

Purpose:
1. To identify and appreciate the communication skills and strategies used in maintaining friendships.

Directions:
1. Watch a television program or series of episodes that show the interaction of friends such as *Friends, ER, Grey's Anatomy, How I Met Your Mother*, or *Desperate Housewives.*
2. Observe the communication skills and strategies listed below used on the show.
3. Observe the impact of these behaviors on the other people and the relationships.

Describe the program and the characters involved. _____

_____

_____

_____

Describe any **expressions of emotions**: _____

_____

_____

Impact: _____

_____

_____

Describe any **relationship talk**: _____

_____

_____

Impact: _____

_____

_____

Describe any **tolerance or restraint**: _____

_____

_____

Impact: _____

_____

_____

Describe any **collaborative conflict efforts**:

_____

_____

_____

Impact: _____

_____

_____

Describe any **comforting or social support**: _____

_____

_____

Impact: _____

_____

_____

Describe any **other-oriented behaviors**: _____

_____

_____

Impact: _____

_____

_____

Describe the **openness, especially self-disclosure**: _____

_____

_____

Impact: _____

_____

_____

Questions:

1. What skills and strategies had the greatest positive impact on the friendships? Why?

2. What lack of skills and strategies had the greatest negative impact on the friendships? Why?

3. How did those relationships that were the strongest compare to those that were the weakest in terms of the communication skills and strategies?

4. What differences (if any) did you observe between men and women in the use of communication skills and strategies for maintaining relationships?

5. What intercultural differences, if any, did you observe in the use of the communication skills and strategies?

EXERCISE 10.8   RECOGNIZING YOUR EMOTIONS

Purpose:
1. To help you identify the emotions you experience.
2. To help you identify how you deal with your emotions.
3. To make you aware of how your emotions affect you and your relationships.

Directions:
1. Observe your thoughts, feelings, and behaviors for several days.
2. Fill in the appropriate spaces on the form below.

Emotion(s)	What were the circumstances? Who else involved?	How did you recognize the emotions?	What did you do? (Verbally and nonverbally)	What affect was there on others?
1.				
2.				
3.				

Emotion(s)	What were the circumstances? Who else involved?	How did you recognize the emotions?	What did you do? (Verbally and nonverbally)	What affect was there on others?
4.				
5.				

Questions:

1. What emotions do you feel most often? In what circumstances and with what people?

2. How do you recognize you emotions?

3. In what ways do you deal with your emotions?

4. How does your emotional state affect your behavior?

5. How does your emotional behavior affect your relationships with others?

6. In what ways would you like to change your emotional communication behaviors?

EXERCISE 10.9   EXPRESSING EMOTIONS

Purpose:
1. To investigate how comfortable you are at expressing emotions in a variety of relationships.

Directions:
1. Think of a specific person that fits each of the following categories and then put the first name of each as the column header for the chart below:
    a. A same-sex acquaintance. (SSA).
    b. An opposite-sex acquaintance. (OSA).
    c. A same-sex friend. (SSF).
    d. An opposite-sex friend. (OSF).
    e. A close same-sex friend. (CSSF).
    f. A close opposite-sex friend. (COSF).
    g. A same-sex parent or relative. (SSP or SSR).
    h. An opposite-sex parent or relative. (OSP or OSR).
2. Indicate how comfortable you would be telling the other person that you are experiencing the specified emotion using the following scale:

Very uncomfortable							**Very comfortable**		
1	**2**	**3**	**4**	**5**	**6**	**7**	**8**	**9**	**10**

Names _____ _____ _____ _____ _____ _____ _____ _____

	SSA	OSA	SSF	OSF	CSSF	COSF	SSP/R	OSP/R
Your Feeling								
Liking for the person								
Love for the person								
Anger with the person								
Disap-point-ment with the person								
Liking for a third person								
Love for a third person								
Anger toward a third person								

Names _____ _____ _____ _____ _____ _____ _____

	SSA	OSA	SSF	OSF	CSSF	COSF	SSP/R	OSP/R
Disappointment with a third person								
Anger toward self								
Disappointment in self								
Embarrassment								
Your fears								
Happy								
Excitement								
Pride								
Uncertainty								

Questions:

1. With whom are you most comfortable sharing your emotions?

2. Which emotions are you most open about?

3. Which emotions are you most closed about?

4. What makes you uncomfortable about sharing certain emotions?

5. Which emotions do you consider to be negative feelings? Positive?

EXERCISE 10.10   ASSESSING SKILLS THAT HAVE HELPED SUSTAIN RELATIONSHIPS.

Purpose:
1. To examine what skills you have applied previously to help maintain a relationship.
2. To examine what skills were absent in relationships that have ended.

Directions:
1. Think of two relationships: one which you have had for a while that continues to be satisfying; and one in which a choice (not dictated by circumstances) was made to end it even though you would have liked it to continue.
2. Go through each checklist and mark those skills and strategies that you were effective in using in each of the two relationships.

Skills/ Strategies	The sustained relationship	The discontinued relationship
1. Effectively communicated your attraction.	_____	_____
2. Effectively cultivated the other's attraction	_____	_____
3. Were open and self-disclosed appropriately.	_____	_____
4. Gathered information to reduce uncertainties	_____	_____
5. Monitored biases and checked perceptions.	_____	_____
6. Listened actively and responded confirmingly.	_____	_____
7. Socially decentered; adapted to your partner.	_____	_____
8. Effectively and openly expressed emotions.	_____	_____
9. Provided comfort and social support	_____	_____
10. Engaged in relationship talk.	_____	_____
11. Was tolerant and appropriately restrained.	_____	_____
12. Managed conflict cooperatively	_____	_____
TOTAL SKILLS/STRATEGIES EFFECTIVELY APPLIED:	_____	_____

Questions

1. In what ways have the skills and strategies contributed to sustaining the relationship?

2. What impact did the presence or absence of skills and strategies have on the discontinued relationship?

3. What differences are there between the sustained and discontinued relationship in terms of what skills and strategies you used?

4. What contributed to those differences?

5. What similarities are there in what skills and strategies were used?

6. Why did some skills and strategies help sustain one relationship and not help the other?

7. If there are any skills or strategies you haven't used in either relationship, explain why you haven't used them.

EXERCISE 10.11   AFFINITY SEEKING

Purpose:
1. To identify your use of affinity seeking strategies for different relationships.
2. To explore alternative affinity seeking strategies you might use.

Directions:
1. Think of two specific people, one you barely know but are attracted to, and the other a casual friend with whom you would like to become closer.
1. Identify which of the eight strategies you use the most by putting an "M" in the space provided for each of the two types of relationships.
2. Identify which strategies you use the least/not at all by putting an "L" for each of the two types of relationships.

	Someone you just met and are attracted to	A casual friend you would like to become closer to
Control: Present yourself as in control, independent, free-thinking, having the ability to reward the other.	_____	_____
Visibility: Increase your visibility to the other person, dress attractively, be interesting & energetic.	_____	_____
Mutual Trust: Display honesty, trustworthiness, reliability, show trust by disclosing.	_____	_____
Politeness: Follow appropriate conversational rules; let the other assume control of the interaction.	_____	_____
Concern and Caring: Show interest, ask questions, listen, show support, be sensitive.	_____	_____
Other-involvement: Draw the other into your activities; display nonverbal immediacy.	_____	_____
Self-involvement: Arrange encounters & interactions; engage in behaviors to encourage a closer relationship.	_____	_____
Commonalities: Point out similarities; Establish equality; display comfort & ease around the other.	_____	_____

Questions:

1. To what degree do the lists show you as being versatile or restricted in your use of the strategies? Why do you suppose that is the case?

2. Explain why you had differences (if you did) in your use of strategies for one relationship type and not for the other.

3. Why don't you use the strategies that you have listed as "L"?

Optional: Try to use one or two of the strategies that you have listed as "L" with either or both of the individuals you identified for this exercise.

4. How did you feel enacting that strategy/those strategies?

5. What was the impact of using that strategy/those strategies?

EXERCISE 10.12 REDUCING RELATIONAL UNCERTAINTIES

Purpose:
1. To identify and manage uncertainties in your relationships.

Directions:
1. Think of three people, one casual friend, one closer friend of the opposite sex, and one very close friend.
2. Evaluate the level of uncertainty you have with the person and his or her views of the relationship by putting a numbering the blanks following each area for potential uncertainty using the following scale:

    0 = no uncertainty
    1 = some uncertainty
    2 = a lot of uncertainty

Source of Potential Uncertainty	Casual Friend	Closer Opposite Sex Friend	Very Close Friend
1. Topics to avoid	_____	_____	_____
2. Topics this person likes to discuss	_____	_____	_____
3. My behaviors that bother this person	_____	_____	_____
4. This person's expectations for the relationship	_____	_____	_____
5. Things that annoy this person	_____	_____	_____
6. Things that please this person	_____	_____	_____
7. This person's feelings toward the relationship	_____	_____	_____
8. This person's view of the future of the relationship	_____	_____	_____
9. What this person wants from the relationship	_____	_____	_____
10. This person's goals in life	_____	_____	_____
11. This person's fears	_____	_____	_____
12. This person's personal strengths	_____	_____	_____
13. This person's personal weaknesses	_____	_____	_____
14. Uncertainties this person has about you.	_____	_____	_____

Questions:

1. Look at uncertainties that go across the relationship types. Why do you suppose you have this pattern of uncertainty in relationships?

2. What can you do to help reduce the uncertainties that run across relationship types?

3. Examine any uncertainties that exist in your closer or very close relationships.
    A. What impact do those uncertainties have on you?

    B. What impact do those uncertainties have on the relationship?

4. Examine your areas of uncertainty.
    A. How comfortable would you feel directly asking the other person for information to reduce that uncertainty?

    B. How appropriate or inappropriate would it be to directly ask for information on those areas of uncertainty?

    C. How is the other person likely to react to a direct request for information on that uncertainty? (Realize this question, in and of itself, is a type of uncertainty you might have).

EXERCISE 10.13   BEING TOLERANT AND SHOWING RESTRAINT

Purpose:
1. To understand how tolerance and restraint help maintain relationships.
2. To identify your own tendencies to be tolerant and restrained.

Directions:
1. Identify the four events described and provide appropriate analysis.

Tolerant Event #1: Describe a situation in which you held back your comment, judgment, disagreement, or criticism.

What impact did your tolerance and restraint have?

Tolerant Event # 2: Describe another situation in which you held back your comment, judgment, disagreement, or criticism.

What impact did your tolerance and restraint have?

Intolerant Event #1: Describe a situation in which you displayed intolerance or lack of restrain in your comments by being judgmental, disagreeing, or criticizing

What impact did your intolerance and lack of restraint have?

Intolerant Event #2: Describe a situation in which you displayed intolerance or lack of restrain in your comments by being judgmental, disagreeing, or criticizing

What impact did your intolerance and lack of restraint have?

Turning Point	Relational Development
Reflective Turning Point	Causal TurningPoint
Relational Escalation	Introductions
Casual Banter	Relational De-escalation
Filtering	Post-Intimacy Relationship
Social Exchange Theory	Immediate Costs and Rewards

Movement of a relationship from one stage to another, either toward or away from greater intimacy	Specific event or interaction associated with positive or negative changes in a relationship.
Event that brings about a change in a relationship.	Event that signals that a change has occurred in the way a relationship is defined.
Sub-stage of the acquaintance stage of relationship development, in which interaction is routine and basic information is shared.	Movement of a relationship toward intimacy through five stages: pre-interaction awareness, acquaintance, exploration, intensification, and intimacy.
Movement of a relationship away from intimacy through five stages: turmoil or stagnation, de-intensification, individualization, separation, and post-separation.	Sub-stage of the acquaintance stage of relational development, in which impersonal topics are discussed but very limited personal information is shared.
Formerly intimate relationship that is maintained at a less intimate stage.	Process of reducing partners moving to each stage by applying selection criteria.
Rewards and costs that are associated with a relationship at the present moment.	Theory that claims people make relationship decisions by assessing and comparing the costs and rewards.

Forecasted Costs and Rewards	Expected Rewards and Costs
Cumulative Rewards and Costs	Affinity Seeking Strategies
Dialectical Theory	Relationship Talk
Uncertainty Reduction Theory	

Expectation of how much reward we should get from a given relationship in comparison to its costs.	Rewards and costs that an individual assumes will occur, based on projection and prediction.
Strategies for getting other people to like you.	Total rewards and costs accrued during a relationship.
Talk about the nature, quality, direction, or definition of a relationship.	Theory that relational development occurs in conjunction with various tensions that exist in all relationships, particularly connectedness versus autonomy, predictability versus novelty, and openness versus closedness.
	Theory that claims people seek information in order to reduce uncertainty, thus providing control and predictability.

CHAPTER 11
MANAGING RELATIONSHIP CHALLENGES

OBJECTIVES

After studying this chapter in the text, *Interpersonal Communication: Relating to Others*, and completing the exercises in this section of the study guide, you should understand:

1. Violations of relational expectations and failure events.
2. How relationships are affected by physical separation and distance.
3. How some relationships face social mores.
4. The types of deception and their impact on relationships.
5. The nature of messages that are hurtful.
6. The nature of obsessive relational intrusion (ORI) and stalking.
7. The nature and impact of jealousy on relationships.
8. Relational violence as the dark side of interpersonal relationships.
9. Ways of responding to relational problems.
10. How ending a relationship follows one of three paths.
11. The general and specific causes for breakups.
12. The elements in Duck's model for ending a relationship.
13. Direct and indirect strategies for ending relationships.\
14. Steps toward postdissolution recovery.

STUDY QUESTIONS

You should be able to answer the following questions:

1. Describe the types of accounts might be provided after a failure event.
2. In what ways does physical separation and distance affect relationships?
3. What types of relationships challenge social norms?
4. Distinguish between deception by omission and deception by commission.
5. What are the three categories for how people react to hurtful messages?
6. What is obsessive relational intrusion?
7. Discuss the nature of relational violence.
8. What are the alternatives for responding to relational problems?
9. What are the main causes of de-escalation and termination?
10. What are the three paths of declining relationships?
11. What are the four phases identified in Duck's model for ending relationships?
12. What are the indirect and direct strategies for ending relationships?
13 . Describe some of the strategies for recovering from a terminated relationship.

EXERCISE 11.1   VIOLATING RELATIONAL EXPECTATIONS: FAILURE EVENTS

Purpose:
1. To become sensitive to instances where you have violated a relational expectation and created a failure event.

Directions:
1. Think about five instances where you have been reproached for violating a relational expectation (created a failure event).
2. Describe the reproach, your account, and your partner's response to the account.
3. Rank order the five events from most severe (1) to least severe (5)

	Brief description of the reproach	Brief description of your account	Response to your account	Rank order
1				
2				
3				
4				
5				

Questions:

1. What factors influenced the severity of the violation (failure event) in the perception of your partners?

2. What types of accounts did you give that were the **most** effective at resolving the situation?

3. What types of accounts did you give that were the **least** effective at resolving the situation?

4. A. To what degree was forgiveness sought or given in any of the failure events?

   B. To what degree was retaliation a factor in any of the failure events?

5. In what ways did the other people's reproaches aggravate you and your accounts?

6. If you could do any of your accounts over again, what would you do differently? Why?

EXERCISE 11.2   ESTABLISHING RULES FOR FRIENDSHIPS

Purpose:

1. To identify the rules you have for friendships.
2. To understand that other people define friendship differently than you do.
3. To recognize that the violating the rules creates failure events.

Directions:

1. Make a list of the rules you have for your friendships; for example, "I expect a friend to keep a secret," "I expect a friend to be there when I need him/her," or "Give each other time to be with other friends."
2. Ask two other people, preferably acquaintances and not friends, to make lists of the rules they have for friendships.
3. Show your list of rules to the other people, and ask them to identify any of your rules that they would find difficult to abide by in a friendship.

My Rules For Friendships

1. _____

2. _____

3. _____

4. _____

5. _____

Person # 1's Rules For Friendships

1. _____

2. _____

3. _____

4. _____

5. _____

Person # 2's Rules For Friendships

1. _____

2. _____

3. _____

4. _____

5. _____

Questions:

1. A. What rules do you have in common or overlap with the other people?

    B. What impact would this have on a developing friendship between you?

2. A. What rules are likely to cause relational problems?

    B. What could be done to help reduce these problems?

4. How do the rules you identified relate to any failure events you've experienced?

5. Which rules from the other people are you likely to violate and thus create a failure event?

EXERCISE 11.3   ASSESSING LONG-DISTANCE RELATIONSHIPS

Purpose:
1. To analyze and understand the dynamics of maintaining long-distance interpersonal relationships.

Directions:
1. Think about two people with whom you have had face-to-face friendships in which one or both of you moved at least 100 miles away; one which you have sustained and one which has terminated by fading away.
2. Fill in the requested information about each of the resulting Long Distance Relationships (LDR).

	THE SUSTAINED FRIENDSHIP	THE FRIENDSHIP THAT FADED AWAY
How close was the relationship before LDR?		
What did you enjoy **most** about this relationship before it became a LDR?		
What did you enjoy **least** about this relationship before it became a LDR?		
What do you or did you enjoy the **most** once it became an LDR?		
What do you or did you enjoy the **least** once it became an LDR?		
What would you like from the friendship that you're not able to get?		
What costs are/were associated with the distance?		
What are/were the greatest challenges you faced because of the distance?		

Questions:
1. Why has the one relationship continued and the other faded away?

2. How have you felt about the relationship that faded away?

EXERCISE 11.4   **INTERVIEWING NON-CONVENTIONAL COUPLES**

Purpose:
1. To appreciate relationships that challenge social norms.
2. To understand the role communication plays in sustaining such relationships.

Directions:
1. For this exercise you need to find an individual who is part of a romantic couple that challenges social norms because the partners are either of different race or ethnicity, have significant age differences, or are of the same sex. You don't have to be friends with the person and might choose to approach a student you know casually who falls within one of these categories.
2. Explain to the person that you would like to interview him or her about his or her relationship for this course, and that you will not be using any names.
3. Interview the person using the following questions:

Interview Questions and Responses
1. Briefly describe how this relationship began?

2. How have other people (friends? family? strangers?) reacted to your relationship?

3. What problems have you encountered with your partner because of your differences (or similarities for gays/lesbians) as the relationship has progressed?

4. What problems have you encountered from other people because of your differences (or similarities for gays/lesbians) as your relationship has progressed?

5. How have you addressed those problems?

Exercise Questions

1. What was the most surprising thing you learned from this person?

2. What factors do you see as making the most contribution to the success of this relationship?

3. In what ways has communication contributed to the development and maintenance of this relationship?

4. What did you learn from this person that might be applicable to your own effectiveness in developing and maintaining relationships?

EXERCISE 11.5   **DECEPTION AS PORTRAYED ON TV**

Purpose:
1. To identify the different types of deception.
2. To understand the impact of deception on relationships.

Directions:
1. Watch a TV comedy or soap opera to find examples for each of the following types of deception or draw upon your memory of previous shows to identify and example of each type of deception.

Concealment

The TV show:

Describe the Incident

Reason for the Deception

Ultimate Impact

White Lies

The TV show:

Describe the Incident

Reason for the Deception

Ultimate Impact

Exaggeration

The TV show:

Describe the Incident

Reason for the Deception

Ultimate Impact

Baldfaced Lie

The TV show:

Describe the Incident

Reason for the Deception

Ultimate Impact

Questions

1. Describe any situations in which you felt the deception was justified and explain your reasoning. If you don't feel any were justified, why not?

2. Which lie had the most negative impact? Why?

3. For those deceptions that were uncovered, explained what lead to their discovery?

EXERCISE 11.6   **MESSAGES THAT HURT YOUR FEELINGS**

Purpose:
1. To understand some of the factors that influence hurtful messages.

Directions:
1. Think of three recent messages that hurt your feelings and complete the questions below.

Message #1 That Hurt Your Feelings
What was said?

By whom and what is his or her relationship to you?

What was the speaker's intention?

How did you react to the speaker? (active verbal, acquiescent, or invulnerable)

Why did it hurt your feelings?

Message #2 That Hurt Your Feelings
What was said?

By whom and what is his or her relationship to you?

What was the speaker's intention?

How did you react to the speaker? (active verbal, acquiescent, or invulnerable)

Why did it hurt your feelings?

Message #3 That Hurt Your Feelings

What was said?

By whom and what is his or her relationship to you?

What was the speaker's intention?

How did you react to the speaker? (active verbal, acquiescent, or invulnerable)

Why did it hurt your feelings?

Questions

1. Rank order the three messages in terms of which one hurt the most to least. What made one hurt more than the others? (relationship, topic, intention, etc.)

2. What commonalities (if any) are there among the types of messages that hurt your feelings?

3. What can you do to reduce such hurtful messages in the future?

EXERCISE 11.7   JEALOUSY

Purpose:
1.   To understand jealousy and its impact on relationships.

Directions:
1. Jealousy is "a reaction to a threat of losing a valued relationship a person believes he or she has." Jealousy is not just limited to romantic relationships but can be any concern we have about the loss or reduction in interaction associated with any relationship; a friend spending less time with you, a family member moving away, a colleague who no longer has time to chat with you.

2. Think about three relationships you have been in over the last couple of years where you have faced concerns about loosing the relationship or it becoming less intimate and complete the following:

1) Partner's first name: _____ Nature of the relationship _____

Behaviors or circumstances
that aroused jealousy:

Your emotional and
behavioral reaction:

Impact on your
communication:

Partner's reaction to
your reaction or feelings:

Ultimate impact on
the relationship:

2) Partner's first name: _____ Nature of the relationship _____

Behaviors or circumstances
that aroused jealousy:

Your emotional and
behavioral reaction:

Impact on your
communication:

Partner's reaction to
your reaction or feelings:

Ultimate impact on
the relationship:

3) Partner's first name: _____ Nature of the relationship _____

Behaviors or circumstances
that aroused jealousy:

Your emotional and
behavioral reaction:

Impact on your
communication:

Partner's reaction to
your reaction or feelings:

Ultimate impact on
the relationship:

Questions:

1. What relationship is there between the nature of your reaction and your partner's reaction to your jealousy?

2. What relationship is there between the nature of your reaction and the ultimate impact on the communication and the relationship?

3. In what ways did your jealousy either improve or diminish the relationship?

4. What other ways might you have reacted to the jealousy?

EXERCISE 11.8   **RELATIONAL VIOLENCE: VERBAL ABUSE**

<u>**Purpose:**</u>
1. Examine the manner in which communication might be used as a form of relational abuse and violence.

<u>**Directions:**</u>
1. Relational violence includes a range of destructive behaviors aimed at other people, including aggressiveness, threats, violent acts, and verbal, psychological, or physical abuse. For this exercise the focus will only be on the manner in which interpersonal communication can be used as a destructive behavior.
2. For each of the following forms of potential verbal abuse, provide one example that you experienced as either the recipient or instigator.

*   Teasing: _____

    _____

*   Intimidating comment: _____

    _____

*   Comment to humiliate: _____

    _____

*   Insults: _____

    _____

*   Degrading comment: _____

    _____

*   Unreasonable demand: _____

    _____

*   Put-down: _____

    _____

*   Comment to embarrass: _____

    _____

*   Name-Calling or racist or sexist remarks: _____

    _____

*   Aggressive communication: _____

    _____

*   Threat to reveal secrets or end relationship: _____

    _____

*   Verbal threat of retaliation or harm: _____

    _____

Questions:

1. Which examples of verbal abuse were easiest to identify? Why?

2. Which examples of verbal abuse were most difficult to identify? Why?

3. A) For those where you were the recipient, which had the least impact on you? Why?

    B) How did you respond?

4. A) For those where you were the recipient, which had the most devastating effects? Why?

    B) How did you respond?

    C) How would you change your response if you had it to do over?

5. In general, for those where you were the instigator, what were your intentions?

6. For those where you were the instigator, how might you have responded in a less verbally abusive manner?

EXERCISE 11.9 **LOSING FRIENDS AND LOVERS**

Purpose:
1. To help you become aware of the reasons you have lost some friends or romantic partners.

Directions:
1. Identify four of friendships and/or romantic relationships that are have ended.
2. List the reasons that each of the relationships ended.

FRIENDSHIP/ROMANTIC RELATIONSHIP #1

Describe the relationship:

_____

_____

State the reasons the relationship ended:

_____

_____

FRIENDSHIP/ROMANTIC RELATIONSHIP #2

Describe the relationship:

_____

_____

State the reasons the relationship ended:

_____

_____

FRIENDSHIP/ROMANTIC RELATIONSHIP #3

Describe the relationship:

_____

_____

State the reasons the relationship ended:

_____

_____

FRIENDSHIP/ROMANTIC RELATIONSHIP #4

Describe the relationship:

_____

_____

State the reasons the relationship ended:

_____

_____

Questions:

1. Which reasons for ending the relationships were the same?

2. Which reasons for ending the relationship were different?

3. What reasons seemed to be the most acceptable? Most unacceptable? Why?

4. If you included both friendships and romantic relationships, what was similar or different about the reasons they ended?

5. Were the reasons you listed the same ones you had immediately after the relationship ended? If not, how did they change? If yes, which reasons do you suspect are the least valid and why?

6. What might have been done to preserve each of the relationships?

EXERCISE 11.10   ENDING YOUR RELATIONSHIPS

<u>**Purpose:**</u>
1.   To become aware of how and why relationships end.
2.   To determine which strategies you use when ending a relationship.
3.   To investigate the reasons your relationships ended.

<u>**Directions:**</u>
1.   Think about a previous relationship (friendship) which <u>**you**</u> terminated.
2.   Think about another relationship which <u>**your partner**</u> terminated.
3.   Fill out the forms below with information about the ending of each relationship.

<u>**RELATIONSHIP #1—One which you initiated the termination.**</u>
Describe the relationship _____

_____

What type of ending did your relationship have? (Circle one of the choices below)
        Faded away   Sudden death   Incrementalism

Explain why the relationship ended the way it did. _____

_____

Which of the following strategies did you use to end the relationship: **Withdrawal,
Pseudo de-escalation, Cost escalation, Negative Identity Management, Justification,
De-escalation, Positive Tone?** What did you say or do?_____

_____

_____

How did your partner react to the strategy (ies)? _____

_____

How did you feel using the strategy (ies)? _____

_____

Why did you end the relationship? _____

_____

What would your partner say was the reason the relationship ended? _____

_____

<u>**RELATIONSHIP #2—One in which your partner initiated termination.**</u>
Describe the relationship _____

_____

What type of ending did your relationship have? (Circle one of the choices below)
Faded away   **Sudden death**   **Incrementalism**

Explain why you believe the relationship ended the way it did _____

_____

Which of the following strategies did you use to end the relationship: **Withdrawal, Pseudo de-escalation, Cost escalation, Negative Identity Management, Justification, De-escalation, Positive Tone?** What did you say or do?_____

_____

_____

How did you react to your partner's strategy (is)? _____

_____

How do you think your partner felt about using the strategy (is)? _____

_____

Why to you think your partner end the relationship? _____

_____

<u>Questions</u>:
1. A. What differences were there in how the two relationships ended?

    B. What contributed to these differences?

2. A. How did your partner's choice of strategy affect you?

    B. How do you think your choice of strategy affected your partner?

3. How satisfied were you with the ending of each of these relationships? Why?

4. If you could do it over again, what would you do differently? Why?

Failure Event	Reproach
Account	In-Group
Deception by Omission (Concealment)	Out-Group
Deception by Commission	White Lie
Exaggeration	Baldfaced Lie
Active Verbal Responses	Acquiescent Responses

Message that a failure event has occurred.	Violations of understandings between people in relationships.
One's racial or ethnic group.	Response to a reproach.
A race, culture, religion, or ethnic group different from one's own.	Intentionally holding back some of the information another person has requested or that you are expected to share.
Deception by commission involving only a slight degree of falsification that has a minimal consequence.	Deliberate presentation of false information.
Deception by commission involving outright falsification of information intended to deceive the listener.	Deception by commission involving "stretching the truth" or embellishing the facts.
Crying, conceding, or apologizing in response to a hurtful message.	Reactive statement made in response to a hurtful message.

Invulnerable Responses	Obsessive Relational Intrusion (ORI)
Stalking	Jealousy
Relational Violence	Bilateral Dissolution
Fading Away	Unilateral Dissolution
Incrementalism	Sudden Death
Intrapsychic Phase	Dyadic Phase

Repeated invasion of a person's privacy by a stranger or acquaintance who desires or assumes a close relationship.	Ignoring, laughing, or being silent in response to a hurtful message.
A reaction to the threat of losing a valued relationship.	Repeated, unwelcome intrusions that create concern for personal safety and fear in the target.
Ending of a relationship by mutual agreement of both parties.	Range of destructive behaviors aimed at other people, including aggressiveness, threats, violent acts, and verbal, psychological, or physical abuse.
Ending of a relationship by one partner, even though the other partner wants it to continue.	Ending a relationship by slowly drifting apart.
Abrupt and unplanned ending of a relationship.	Systematic progression of a relationship through each of the de-escalation stages.
Second phase in relationship termination, when the individual discusses termination with the partner.	First phase in relationship termination, when an individual engages in an internal evaluation of the partner

Social Phase	Grave Dressing Phase
Direct Relational Termination Strategies	Indirect Relational Termination Strategies

Final phase in relationship termination, when the partners generate public explanations and move past the relationship.	Third phase in relationship termination, when members of the social network around both parties are informed of and become involved in the termination process.
Attempts to break up a relationship without explicitly stating the desire to do so.	Explicit statements of a desire to break up a relationship.

CHAPTER 12
INTERPERSONAL RELATIONSHIPS AT HOME, THROUGH COMPUTER-MEDIATED COMMUNICATION, AND AT WORK

OBJECTIVES

After studying the material in this chapter of *Interpersonal Communication: Relating to Others* and completing the exercises in this section of the study guide, you should understand:

1. The definition of family and the difference between the natural, blended, single parent, and extended families.
2. The significance of the cohesion and adaptability model of family functioning.
3. How to improve family relationships by using the communication characteristics of a healthy family.
4. How CMC compares to face-to-face communication.
5. The development of relationships solely through computer-mediated communication CMC)
6. How CMC can be used to enhance Face-to-Face (FtF) relationships.
7. The dark side of CMC—cyberstalking, harassment, and compulsion.
8. Interpersonal communication skills that can facilitate effective CMC.
9. The nature of workplace friendships and romances.
10. The difference between upward, downward, horizontal, and outward communication.

STUDY QUESTIONS

You should be able to answer the following questions:

1. What is a family?
2. How are the four types of families described?
3. How does the Circumplex Model of Family Systems show that adaptability and cohesion interact to create different family types?
4. What skills and strategies can be used to improve family communication?
5. What is meant by social or psychological co-presence and hyperpersonal relationships?
6. In what ways does compute-mediated communication differ from face-to-face interactions?
7. Describe how CMC can lead to the formation of new relationships.
8. Describe the role of CMC in escalating and maintaining FtF relationships?
9. Explain the dark side of CMC.
10. Describe the communication skills needed for effective CMC.
11. Why are workplace friendships and romances important to us?
12. What does *quid pro quo* and *hostile environment* mean?
13. What is the difference between upward, downward, horizontal, and outward communication in organizations?

EXERCISE 12.1   YOUR SENSE OF FAMILY

Purpose:
1.   To appreciate the nuisances of defining family and identifying them.

Directions:
1.   Complete the questionnaire below indicating whether you personally regard each relationship described as constituting a "family."
2.   Provide a brief rationale to support your decision.

Which is a "Family"?		Brief Rationale
1. A person living by her/himself	Y___ N___	
2. A man and a woman living together with <u>independent</u> financial arrangement	Y___ N___	
3.. A husband and a wife living together	Y___ N___	
4. A husband and wife separated	Y___ N___	
5. A homosexual couple living together	Y___ N___	
6. A husband, wife, and child living together	Y___ N___	
7. A homosexual couple, and child together	Y___ N___	
8. A woman and her child living together	Y___ N___	
9. A man and his grandson, living together	Y___ N___	
10. Two brothers living together	Y___ N___	
11. A group of people living together that refers to themselves as a family	Y___ N___	
12. A father living in one place, a mother in another, and their kids elsewhere	Y___ N___	
13. Two best friends who have shared an apartment for 10 years.	Y___ N___	
14. Newlyweds, right after their wedding	Y___ N___	

Directions Continued
3.   The text defines family as "a self-defined unit made up of any number of persons who live or have lived in a relationship with one another over time in a common living space and who are usually, but not always, united by marriage or kinship." Decide which are families according to this definition and record your answer in a different color of ink/pencil.

4. Read the list to someone who has not taken this class and ask him or her to identify which are families and which are not and record his or her responses and discuss any differences.

Questions:

1. What were the general criteria in your own conceptualization of a family that you used in making your initial evaluations?

2. What qualities were missing from those you identified as not being families?

3. According to your criteria, what would a definition of a family be?

4. In what ways does your definition differ from that in the text?

5. What factors in your life have influenced your conceptualization of a family?

6. A) Discuss the differences and similarities between your responses and your friends?

   B) What probably contributed to your differences?

EXERCISE 12.2   INVESTIGATING YOUR FAMILY RULES

Purpose:
1. To help you become aware of how your family rules, roles, patterns, traditions, and norms evolved.

Directions:
1. Reflect back on the family in which you grew up.
2. Answer the following questions about communication behavior by stating a rule your family had in regard to the question.

What topics could not be talked about openly? ("Never discuss sex with Dad.")

_____

_____

_____

How did your family handle conflict situations? ("Do as I say, not as I do.")

_____

_____

_____

Whom did you talk to about serious matters? ("Mom listens better than Dad.")

_____

_____

_____

Who talked to whom and when could they talk? ("The boys talked to Mom and the girls talked to Dad.")

_____

_____

_____

In what circumstances did subgroups or hierarchies appear to form in your family? ("When you want to get your way, go to Mom and Dad with at least one sibling.")

_____

_____

_____

How comfortable were your family members with touching behavior? ("Don't go to bed without kissing Mom and Dad.")

_____

_____

_____

How would you describe the communication patterns, in general, in your family--closed, open, sarcastic, friendly and warm, etc.? (Sarcastic humor covers hidden feelings.)

_____

_____

_____

What language (words or phrases) was not accepted? (No profanity allowed.)

_____

_____

_____

What rules did you have about eye contact? ("Look at me when I am talking to you!")

_____

_____

_____

What rules were there regarding voice? ("No screaming in the house.")

_____

_____

_____

What rules existed about clothing and appearance? ("Take off your shoes at the door.")

_____

_____

_____

Questions:

1. Which of your rules do you still follow within your family? Why?

2. Which rules have changed for you? Why?

3. How did you become aware of each of the rules you mentioned? Who made the rule? Was the rule stated explicitly to you or did you learn it by experience?

4. Which rules will (did) you take with you into your own family?

EXERCISE 12.3   READJUSTING YOUR FAMILY

Purpose:
1. To identify the significant events that have impacted your family interactions.
2. To determine family cohesion and adaptability following these events.

Directions:
1. Under "Number of Occurrences" indicate how many times in the past year each of the events has occurred.
2. Multiply the number under "Scale Value" by the number of occurrences of each event and place the answer under "Your Score."
3. Add the figures under "Your Score" to find your total for the past year.

FAMILY READJUSTMENT SCALE

Your Score	Scale Value	Number of Occurrences	Life Event
_____	100	_____	Death of spouse.
_____	73	_____	Divorce.
_____	65	_____	Marital Separation.
_____	63	_____	Death of a close family member.
_____	53	_____	Personal injury or illness.
_____	50	_____	Marriage.
_____	47	_____	Fired at work.
_____	45	_____	Marital reconciliation.
_____	45	_____	Retirement.
_____	44	_____	Change in health of family member.
_____	40	_____	Pregnancy.
_____	39	_____	Sex difficulties.
_____	39	_____	Gain of new family member.
_____	39	_____	Business readjustment.
_____	38	_____	Change in financial state.
_____	37	_____	Death of a close friend.
_____	36	_____	Change to different line of work.
_____	35	_____	Change in number of arguments with spouse
_____	31	_____	Mortgage over $10,000.
_____	30	_____	Foreclosure of mortgage or loan.
_____	29	_____	Change in responsibilities at work.
_____	29	_____	Son or daughter leaving home.
_____	29	_____	Trouble with in-laws.
_____	28	_____	Outstanding personal achievement.
_____	26	_____	Wife begins or stops work.
_____	26	_____	Begin or end school.
_____	25	_____	Change in living conditions.
_____	24	_____	Revision of personal habits.
_____	23	_____	Trouble with boss.
_____	20	_____	Change in work hours or conditions.

	20		Change in residence.
	20		Change in schools.
	19		Change in recreation.
	19		Change in church activities.
	18		Change in social activities.
	17		Mortgage or loan less than $10,000.
	16		Change in sleeping habits.
	15		Change in number of family get-togethers.
	15		Change in eating habits.
	13		Vacation.
	12		Christmas.
	11		Minor violations of the law.

_____   **This is your total life change score for the past year.**

If you scored at least 150 you have about a 50-50 chance of developing an illness or stress-induced health change. A score above 300 points increases the likelihood of a health change to almost 90 percent.

Questions:

1. How did these events affect your family?

2. How did your family communicate about these events when they were occurring?

3. In what ways has your family demonstrated "adaptability" in responding to these events?

4. In what ways did your family's level of cohesion affect the management of these events?

EXERCISE 12.4   WATCHING TV FAMILIES COMMUNICATE

Purpose:
1. To observe communication patterns in different families.
2. To become aware of healthy and unhealthy communication behaviors in families.

Directions:
1. Choose two television sit-coms that revolve around a family. Choose different family types or different cultural families. The programs may be current or reruns, such as: *Malcolm in the Middle, Everybody Loves Raymond, Full House, Roseanne, Married with Children, Hangin' With Mr. Cooper, Fresh Prince of Bel-Air, Party of Five*, and *7th Heaven.*
2. Describe the family type.
3. Find communication behaviors that illustrate healthy and unhealthy families.

TV SHOW #1:   Name: _____

Describe the type of family:

_____

_____

_____

Communication Patterns

1. Taking time to talk about relationships and feelings.

_____

_____

_____

2. Listening and clarifying the meaning of messages.

_____

_____

_____

3. Supporting and encouraging one another.

_____

_____

_____

Using productive strategies for managing conflict, stress, and change.

_____

_____

_____

TV SHOW #2:   Name: _____

Describe the type of family:

_____

_____

_____

Communication Patterns

1. Talking about relationships and feelings.

_____

_____

_____

2. Listening and clarifying the meaning of messages.

_____

_____

_____

3. Supporting and encouraging one another.

_____

_____

_____

4. Using strategies for managing conflict, stress, and change.

_____

_____

_____

<u>Questions:</u>

1. What similarities were there in communication patterns on the shows you choose?

2. How were they different?

3. What dysfunctional communication behaviors did you observe most often?

4. What healthy communication behaviors were used most frequently?

5. According to the Circumplex Model of Family Systems, what type of families do the two represent? Why?

EXERCISE 12.5   ASSESSING YOUR FAMILY'S COMMUNICATION

Purpose:
1. To become aware what constitutes good, healthy family communication (drawn from the text discussion of Virginia Satir and John Caughlin).
2. To analyze your own family experiences.

Directions:
1. Think of your current family or your family of origin and respond to the following:

FAMILY COMMUNICATION QUESTIONNAIRE

Use the following scale in deciding how much each statement applies to your family:

5) Strongly Agree, 4) Agree, 3) Agree/Disagree, 2) Disagree, 1) Strongly Disagree

_____ 1. My family fosters feelings of high self-worth.

_____ 2. We directly present our ideas and issues to each other.

_____ 3. Family members are specific in their communication to each other.

_____ 4. Family members communicate honestly with each other.

_____ 5. There are rules in my family but they are flexible.

_____ 6. The children in the family were (are) treated as people.

_____ 7. My family displays strong affectionate touching behaviors.

_____ 8. We discuss our fears, hurts, angers, criticism, and disappointments openly.

_____ 9. Family members share the joys they experience.

_____ 10. Our communication is open.

_____ 11. There is structural stability—roles are clear and remain stable.

_____ 12. Family members express their affection for one another.

_____ 13. Family members provide emotional and instrumental support.

_____ 14. We are polite to one another.

_____ 15. Rules for how to behave and the consequences for breaking the rules are clear.

_____ 16 Our family communication is filled with humor and sarcasm.

_____ 17. We take time to talk about our relationships and feelings.

_____ 18. We listen actively and seek clarification of confusing messages.

_____ 19. We support and encourage each other.

_____ 20. We use productive, collaborative strategies to manage conflict and change.

_____ **TOTAL (add the scores for the 20 items)**

Questions:

1. A score of 60 would put your family in the middle of the communication scores.
   A) Discuss your family's total as it relates to this median point.

   B) To what degree does your family score match your view of how effective communication is in your family?

2. Examine any items that you marked with a 1 or 2.
   A) To what degree do these reflect weaknesses in your family's communication?

   B) What might be done to improve these qualities?

3. Of the qualities that were rated strongest for your family, which ones do you think contribute the most to effective communication in your family? Why?

4. Which qualities seem least important to the overall quality of your family communication? Why?

5. As you start (or have started) to form your own family (get married and have kids), which qualities will you strive the most to establish in your household? Why?

EXERCISE 12.6   COMPUTER-MEDIATED COMMUNICATION SURVEY

Purpose:
1. To examine how computer-mediated communication is being used by informally surveying your friends

Directions:
1. Survey at least five friends either face-to-face or online and place a mark in each blank for their answers. Try to get a diverse sample.
2. Don't include any names, but assign each person a number, 1, 2, 3, 4, 5, etc.
3. Put each person's number in the blanks that correspond to his or her responses.

Background Questions
Record some background information on your respondents:

Respondent #1: Sex: _____ Approximate Age: _____ Race: _____ Major/Job: _____

Respondent #2: Sex: _____ Approximate Age: _____ Race: _____ Major/Job: _____

Respondent #3: Sex: _____ Approximate Age: _____ Race: _____ Major/Job: _____

Respondent #4: Sex: _____ Approximate Age: _____ Race: _____ Major/Job: _____

Respondent #5: Sex: _____ Approximate Age: _____ Race: _____ Major/Job: _____

Internet Survey

	Very Often	Often	Some	A little	Never
1. How often to you participate in chat rooms with your friends / or instant message them?	_____	_____	_____	_____	_____
2. How often to you participate in chat rooms with people you don't know?	_____	_____	_____	_____	_____
3. How often do you exchange emails with friends that currently live in the same city as you?	_____	_____	_____	_____	_____
4. How often do you exchange emails with friends that leave in other cities?	_____	_____	_____	_____	_____
5. How often do you exchange emails with family members?	_____	_____	_____	_____	_____
6. How often do you post messages on interest group bulletin boards?	_____	_____	_____	_____	_____

Internet Survey   Responses

	Very Often	Often	Some	A little	Never
7. How often have you been "flamed" while on the Internet?	_____	_____	_____	_____	_____
8. How often do you use "smileys" or emoticons in your messages?	_____	_____	_____	_____	_____
9. How often have you gotten into conflicts with people while using CMC?	_____	_____	_____	_____	_____
10. How often do you use your cell phone for text messaging?	_____	_____	_____	_____	_____

11. Have you ever become friends
with someone you first met
on the Internet?   Yes: _____   No: _____

12. Have you ever had a former
friend harass you through emails or
text messages?   Yes: _____   No: _____

Questions

1. What differences do you see among the respondents based upon their sex, age, race, or major/job?

2. What questions have the greatest amount of similarity among the respondents? Why do you suppose that is?

3. What questions have the greatest among of variation among the respondents? Why do you suppose that is?

4. What conclusions do the survey results suggest about computer-mediated communication and interpersonal relationships?

EXERCISE 12.7   EXPRESSING EMOTIONS ON THE INTERNET: EMOTICONS

Purpose:
1. To examine how people communicate emotions in their computer-mediated messages.

Directions:
1. Log on to a chat room. You can do this through such www locations as chat.yahoo.com or msn.com (Microsoft).
2. Find an active room with lots of people. You don't have to send any messages or respond to messages from others. Simply observe the messages being posted.
3. Record below as many ways as you notice that people are communicating their emotions (using capitalization, exclamation marks, etc.). Record any emoticons that people use along with the emotion it is representing.

Record of Internet Chat Room Emotional Expressions/Emoticons

Emotional Expression/Emoticon   **Emotional Meaning**

1. _____

2. _____

3. _____

4. _____

5. _____

6. _____

7. _____

8. _____

9. _____

10. _____

11. _____

12. _____

Questions:

1. What was the most common way that people expressed emotions?

2. What does your list reflect about the relative expression of positive versus negative emotions?

3. What effect did one person's emotional expression have on other posters?

4. Were there any emoticons you had never seen before? If so, how did you determine what they meant?

5. How did you react to the emotional cues that you saw in the messages? Did any of them evoke an emotional reaction?

6. In general, how satisfied are you with your ability to express your emotions in your CMC? Why?

**EXERCISE 12.8   COMPARING YOUR COMPUTER-MEDIATED
COMMUNICATION (CMC) WITH YOUR
FACE TO FACE (FtF) COMMUNICATION**

Purpose:

1. To examine how your computer-mediated (CMC) interactions compare with your face-to-face (FtF) interactions.

Directions:

1. For each of the statements indicate whether it applies more to your computer-mediated or face-to-face communication. You can also indicate both or neither.

	CMC	FtF
1. I find it easier to disclose about myself.	____	____
2. I disclose more about my emotions.	____	____
3. I feel more comfortable asking questions about the other person.	____	____
4. I enjoy interacting more.	____	____
5. I feel more anxiety interacting with a stranger.	____	____
6. There is more danger in interacting with someone.	____	____
7. I can tell when someone is lying more easily.	____	____
8. I am more anxious about being stalked or harassed.	____	____
9. I draw more accurate impressions of others.	____	____
10. People get a better impression of me.	____	____
11. I find it easier to make plans.	____	____
12. I am more comfortable giving bad news or terminating a relationships.	____	____

Questions:

1. What do your answers reflect about your comfort and preference for computer-mediated communication (CMC) versus face-to-face communication (FtF)?

2. Which two statements most strongly reflected your feelings about the CMC/FtF? Why?

EXERCISE 12.9   COMPUTER-MEDIATED COMMUNICATION IN ON-GOING RELATIONSHIPS

Purpose:
1. To examine how you use computer-mediated communication in an on-going relationship.

Directions:
1. Over the next few days pay attention to your interactions with a friend with whom you have on-going face-to-face (FtF) communication and as well as computer-mediated communication (CMC)(email or instant messaging).
2. Record your responses to the following questions.

Observations:
1. The advantages of your CMC over FtF was:

2. The advantages of FtF over CMC was:

3. In what ways did the information you exchanged differ between FtF and CMC?

4. In what ways was the information you exchanged similar between FtF and CMC?

5. Was there more misunderstanding or confusion in FtF or CMC? What types of misunderstandings or confusion were there?

6. What relational maintenance strategies occurred in your CMC?

7. In what ways did you adapt your CMC to your partner?

EXERCISE 12.10   EVALUATING WORKPLACE FRIENDSHIPS

Purpose:
1.   To understand the affect the workplace friendships have on you.
2.   To compare workplace and non-workplace friendships.

Directions:
1.   Think about your current or most recent work situation while answering the following questions about your relationships with other people at work.

Workplace Relationship Analysis

Describe the closest relationships you formed with any other people at work.

How many friendships do you or did you have at work?

What circumstances affected the formation of these friendships?

What are/were your relative roles at the workplace (co-workers, workers in different departments, supervisor-subordinate, etc.)

How do/did these friendships affect your job performance?

How do/did these friendships affect your job satisfaction?

What types of issues did you typically talk about?

What topics did you intentionally avoid?

How often did you engage in activities with these friends outside of the workplace? What types of activities?

What differences are there between your workplace friendships and your non-workplace friendships?

What similarities are there between your workplace friendships and your non-workplace friendships?

How did conflicts in your workplace friendships affect your work?

Questions

1. Overall, to what degree does your analysis demonstrate that workplace friendships are beneficial or detrimental to workplace performance?

EXERCISE 12.11   RECOGNIZING MESSAGE DIRECTION

Purpose:
1. To identify examples of upward, downward, horizontal, and outward communication in your workplaces. (You can use examples from school or home if the direction of the message fits what's requested.)

Directions:
1. Find two examples of each type of message over the next few days.
2. Identify the relationship between the sender and the receiver.

UPWARD MESSAGES

Sender	Receiver	Content of message

DOWNWARD MESSAGES

Sender	Receiver	Content of message

HORIZONTAL MESSAGES

Sender	Receiver	Content of message

OUTWARD MESSAGES

Sender	Receiver	Content of message

Questions:

1. How did the messages affect the relationships between the senders and the receivers?

_____

_____

_____

EXERCISE 12.12   THE IMPORTANCE OF EMPLOYEE COMMUNICATION SKILLS TO EMPLOYERS

Purpose:
1. To help you become aware of the emphasis from organizations and businesses on competent communication skills.

Directions:
1. Find five advertisements for employment possibilities in an area of interest to you in three different newspapers: (1) your local paper, (2) a national paper such as *Wall Street Journal* or *Washington Post*, and (3) a paper from a major city other than the one in which you live (you can access ads from various papers on-line).
2. Identify the skills and experiences wanted by potential employers, especially notice the communication skills desired.

Questions:

1. What skills are the employers looking for in new employees?

_____

_____

_____

_____

2. What experiences are the employers looking for?

_____

_____

3. What educational background are the employers looking for?

_____

_____

4. What communication skills are requested by employers?

_____

_____

_____

_____

5.   Why do you suppose they have included these skills?

_____

_____

_____

_____

6.   What are the salary ranges for the jobs that you found advertised?

_____

_____

_____

7.   How can you prepare for these job opportunities?

_____

_____

_____

8.   Even if the ads don't specifically ask for interpersonal communication skills, how might such skills be an asset in these positions?

_____

_____

_____

9.   How will this course help you be better prepared for your career?

_____

_____

_____

_____

EXERCISE 12.13   MALE AND FEMALE INTERACTIONS ON-LINE AND AT WORK

Purpose:
1. To explore differences and similarities between men and women's communication in computer-mediated communication and at the workplace.

Directions:
1. Indicate whether you think each item is true or false (T or F) and then ask a friend of the opposite sex the same questions and record his or her answers and then discuss your answers.

Yours / Other's

_____ _____1. You can't tell the difference between men and women by their emails.

_____ _____2. Women express more emotions online than do men.

_____ _____3. Men use email to coordinate activities more than women do.

_____ _____4. Women are more vulnerable in chat rooms than are men.

_____ _____5. Public chat rooms are primarily used by lonely people and perverts.

_____ _____6. You can form close personal relationships on-line without ever meeting face to face.

_____ _____7. Female bosses are harder on their employees than male bosses.

_____ _____8. Female workers are more emotional at work than male workers.

_____ _____9. At work, men are more competitive and power hungry than women.

_____ _____10. Men are more inclined to seek leadership positions, while women prefer to be followers.

_____ _____11. Women are treated as equal to men in the workplace.

_____ _____12. Men and women can have close, platonic friendships with each other in the workplace..

Questions:
1. Assuming your partner's responses are generalizable to his or her sex, how might any differences impact interactions with the opposite sex online and in the workplace?

2. What conclusions can you draw about male-female communication based on the similarity or differences between you and your friend?

EXERCISE 12.2   UNDERSTANDING THE FAMILY AS A SYSTEM

Purpose:
1. To help you understand the family as a communication system.
2. To investigate how your family is interdependent, complex, open, and adaptive.

Directions:
1. Observe your current family or your family of origin.
2. Give an example for each of the aspects of the family system listed below.
3. Explain the communication behavior your family used in each situation described.

FAMILY SYSTEMS ARE INTERDEPENDENT

Describe a situation that happened in your family that affected every member of the family in some way.

_____

_____

_____

How did you communicate?

_____

_____

_____

FAMILY SYSTEMS ARE COMPLEX

Discuss a time when members of your family had different meanings or interpretations of a single event.

_____

_____

_____

How did you communicate?

_____

_____

_____

FAMILY SYSTEMS ARE OPEN

Discuss a time when something that happened outside the family had an impact or influence on the members of the family.

_____

_____

_____

How did you communicate?

_____

_____

_____

FAMILY SYSTEMS ARE ADAPTIVE

Discuss a time when a change took place to which your family had to adjust.

_____

_____

_____

How did you communicate?

_____

_____

_____

	YES	**NO**	**SOMETIMES**
1. Is it difficult for you to converse with other family members?	_____	_____	_____
2. Do you feel other family members lack respect for you?	_____	_____	_____
3. During family discussions, is it difficult for you to admit that you are wrong when you recognize that you are wrong about something?	_____	_____	_____
4. Is it difficult to accept constructive criticism?	_____	_____	_____
5. Do you pretend that you are listening to other family members when you are not really listening?	_____	_____	_____
6. Do you find yourself being inattentive while in a conversation with other family members?	_____	_____	_____
7. When a problem arises between you and another family member, do you become emotionally upset?	_____	_____	_____
8. Are you dissatisfied with the way you settle your disagreements with members of your family?	_____	_____	_____
9. Do you misunderstand other family members?	_____	_____	_____
10. Do you fail to express disagreement with other family members because you are afraid they will get angry?	_____	_____	_____
11. Does it upset you a great deal when another family member disagrees with you?	_____	_____	_____
12. Is it difficult to confide in other family members?	_____	_____	_____
13. Do you feel other family members wish you were a different type of person?	_____	_____	_____
14. Do other family members fail to understand your feelings?	_____	_____	_____

Questions:

1.   What did you learn about your family by doing this exercise?

2.   Which situations turned out well for your family? Not well?

3.   How could you change your communication behaviors to deal with the situations in a more productive, cohesive way?

Family	Natural Family
Blended Family	Single-Parent Family
Extended Family	Family of Origin
Circumplex Model of Family Interaction	Adaptability
Cohesion	Computer-Mediated Communication (CMC)
Synchronous Interaction	Asynchronous Interaction

Mother, father, and their biological children.	Self-defined unit made up of any number of persons who live or have lived in relationship with one another over time in a common living space who are usually, but not always, united by marriage and kinship.
One parent raising one or more children.	Two adults and their children. Because of divorce, separation, death, or adoption, the children may be the offspring of other parents, or of just one of the adults who is raising them.
Family in which a person is raised.	Relatives such as aunts, uncles, cousins, or grandparents and/or unrelated persons who are part of the family unit.
Family's ability to modify and respond to changes in the family's power structure and roles.	Model of the relationships among family adaptability, cohesion, and communication.
Communication between and among people through the medium of computers (includes e-mail, chat rooms, bulletin boards, and newsgroups).	The emotional bonding and feelings of togetherness that families experience.
Interaction in which participants send and receive messages from each other with delays between reception and response.	Interaction in which participants are actively engaging at the same time.

Social or Psychological Co-Presence	Hyperpersonal Relationships
Quid pro quo	Downward Communication
Upward Communication	Hostile Environment
Horizontal Communication	Outward Communication

Relationships formed primarily through CMC (computer-mediated communication) that become more personal than equivalent FtF (Face-to-Face) relationships.	State of mind that occurs during computer-mediated interactions or text messaging, in which partners think and act as though they were face to face.
Communication that flows from superiors to subordinates.	Latin phrase that can be used to describe a type of sexual harassment. The phrase roughly means "You do something for me and I'll do something for you."
Type of sexual harassment in which an employee's rights are threatened through offensive working conditions or behavior on the part of other workers.	Communication that flows from subordinates to superiors.
Communication that flows to those outside an organization (such as customers).	Communication among colleagues or coworkers at the same level within an organization.

NOTES

NOTES

NOTES

NOTES

NOTES

NOTES

NOTES